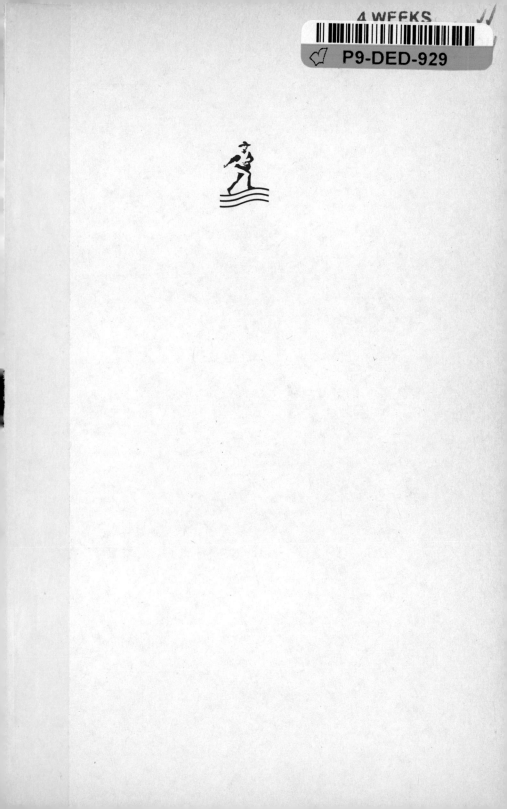

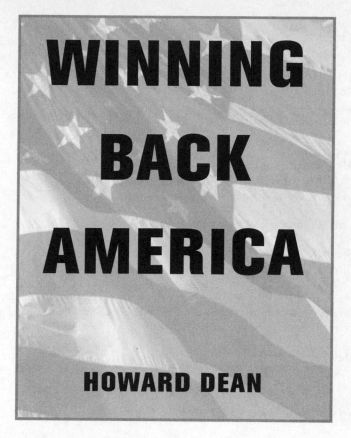

WINNING BACK AMERICA

HOWARD DEAN

Simon & Schuster
New York   London   Toronto   Sydney

SIMON & SCHUSTER
Rockefeller Center
1230 Avenue of the Americas
New York, NY 10020

First Simon & Schuster trade paperback edition 2003

SIMON & SCHUSTER and colophon are registered trademarks of
Simon & Schuster, Inc.

For information regarding special discounts for bulk purchases,
please contact Simon & Schuster Special Sales at 1-800-456-6798
or business@simonandschuster.com

Designed by Helene Berinsky

Manufactured in the United States of America

10   9   8   7   6   5   4   3   2   1

Library of Congress Cataloging-in-Publication Data

Dean, Howard, 1948–
    Winning back America / Howard Dean.
        p.   cm.
        1. Presidents—United States—Election—2004.   2. United
States—Politics and government—2001–   3. Dean, Howard,
1948–   4. Presidential candidates—United States—Biography.
5. Governors—Vermont—Biography.   I. Title.
E905.D43   2003
974.3'044'092—dc22
[B]   2003060529

ISBN 0-7432-5571-2

For Judy, Anne, and Paul

INTRODUCTION

In order to achieve everything we want to achieve, we have to stand up for what we believe in again. Standing up for what we believe means standing together. Restoring the American community is not something that can be done from a podium, or by any person, whether or not he or she is a candidate for public office; it is a goal that requires the active participation in our communities by each of us.

President Bush said time and time again in 2000 that he was "a uniter, not a divider," yet nothing could be further from the truth. His has been a policy of domestic division, and he has sought to advance his political agenda by dividing the American people by race, by gender, by sexual orientation, and by income. Dividing the American people against ourselves is not a sound foundation for governing; and in the end, if we allow such tactics of division to continue, we will not only have lost ground on the issues that we care about, we will have lost a fundamental characteristic of what it means to be an American—the notion that we are all in this together.

On June 23, 2003, as I took the stage on Church Street in downtown Burlington to announce my presidential campaign, I was buoyed by the presence of so many family members, friends, and colleagues. I was thrilled that Vermont's Senators Pat Leahy and Jim Jeffords were there, too. Senators Leahy and Jeffords are terrific people. Pat is one of the consciences of the Senate; as chair of the Judiciary Committee, he fended off a number of inappropriate judicial nominees; he also was responsible for including "sunset clauses" in some of the more onerous parts of the Patriot Act.

Jim Jeffords became a national legend for his willingness to stand up to the president's radical agenda. When Jim left the Republican Party, largely out of frustration with the president's failure to fulfill his promises on education, he exhibited a true Vermont trait—the willingness to do what is right, even when faced with the toughest opposition.

On that stunning early-summer day, I stood in front of more than thirty thousand Americans who had gathered in Burlington and, via the Internet, across the country. Much had changed in the year since I had first begun to travel around the country, listening to the concerns of my fellow Americans, understanding our shared fears, hopes, and aspirations. In many ways, that speech on June 23 was the culmination of what I had learned in a year of listening to the American people.

We were united that day in Vermont and throughout America, and we have been united in common cause and in ever-greater numbers since June 23. Our cause is the Great American Restoration—the restoration of our ideals, of our communities, and of our nation's traditional role as a beacon of hope in the world. All of these have been endangered by the policies of the Bush administration, but the people of America have extraordinary power, and when the American people work together, in common cause, there is nothing that we cannot achieve.

PART ONE

CHAPTER

★ **1** ★

My family comes from Sag Harbor, New York. Our roots in America are very deep; they can be traced back to the eighteenth century. One of my ancestors on my father's mother's side was a whaling captain named Benjamin Huntting. Huntting's daughter married Joseph Fahys, who had come over from France without a penny. Eventually Fahys, my great-great-grandfather, started a watchcase factory, which remains in Sag Harbor to this day. Huntting's place is also still standing—it is now a whaling museum. Later, my grandfather became the first mayor of the town of North Haven, New York.

My father's side of the family has been in the brokerage business in New York City for many years. My father, Howard Brush Dean, Jr., worked for a company called Harris, Upham for twenty-five years, until he left to work for Reynolds and Company, which was taken over by Dean Witter in 1978. (There was no relation—"Dean" was Witter's first name.) My mother is Andrée Maitland Dean. Her grandfather, a Catholic, came to this country from Scotland at a very young age. My heritage has always been important to me: My daughter Anne's middle name is Huntting; my son Paul's is Maitland.

I was born in 1948 at the old Doctors' Hospital in Manhattan, the eldest of four boys. My brother Charlie was born in 1950, and Jim and Bill came along in 1954 and 1955, respectively.

Eventually, my mother's four boys became four teenagers (on top of my father, who was sometimes a teenager at heart). When we got into trouble, we turned to my mother first. If it was something serious, my father was told, but he rarely got mad. Driving, I once took a gravel curve at thirty miles an hour and ran into a pine tree. I was upset, but my father was terrific. "These things happen," he said. On disciplinary matters, however, he ruled the roost with a firm hand.

Although I was born in New York and went to school in the city until I was thirteen, I feel I really grew up in East Hampton on eastern Long Island. East Hampton had its wealthy people from the city who'd come up in the summer, but there were people of every background living there throughout the year. When I was growing up, there were more potato farms than second homes there; Long Island potatoes used to rival those from Maine and Idaho. Every once in a while, we'd sneak a potato or two out of a farmer's field, just to say we'd done it.

Television was never a factor in our upbringing. The only station we could get was Channel 8 out of New Haven, Connecticut, and even that was too fuzzy to watch. Back in New York, we were allowed only one half hour per night. I watched *The Three Stooges* (which my father loved) and some *Abbott & Costello*, but not much was permitted beyond that. I remember that a movie at the Edwards Theater on Main Street in East Hampton cost a quarter if you were under twelve.

For us, it was an idyllic childhood. We were outdoors most of the time. We rode our bikes everywhere and nobody thought anything of it. We spent a lot of time at the beach and around the local duck pond. We went to Montauk on the very eastern end of Long Island and fished for bluefish. In the summer, in particular, the family spent a lot of time on the water, out on Gardiner's Bay, for instance, where we looked for blowfish and striped bass.

The four Dean boys played sports whenever we could. There were always a lot of cousins around, and we played endless pickup games of one kind or another—touch football, basketball, softball, and especially ice hockey. We had a large pond behind our house, and in the winter, we'd get up at 8:30 and be on the ice by 9:30. Other than the time it took for a quick lunch, we'd stay on the ice until dark.

In the summers when I got a little older, we went sailing, we went to local boys' club camps, and played baseball. Once we were eighteen, we could indulge in lazy days of "Baseball and Ballantine." We'd buy some beer and put it in a garbage can of ice and play softball all day long. If you hit somebody's beer with a batted ball, it was an automatic out.

My father was a great role model to his sons. He had friends from all walks of life and was a very down-to-earth person. He belonged to the Maidstone Club, a very exclusive club in East Hampton, but he spent his winters shooting coot with his local childhood friends.

Even though he did very well in business, my father was extremely careful with his finances. We were the only kids on the baseball team who didn't have uniforms (my father thought a uniform was a waste of money because a kid would just grow out of it). We were given an allowance—25 cents a week to start with. When we got to be ten, he switched us to $1 a month. At the time, we thought that was a raise.

From the age of thirteen, I attended St. George's School in Newport, Rhode Island. The school has an incredibly beautiful setting, up on a hill overlooking the Atlantic Ocean. I was happy to get away from the city. It was a chance to play the sports we enjoyed on Long Island all year round.

Although I loved hockey, it turned out that pond hockey is not really enough to make you into a good hockey player, no matter how much of it you play. You've really got to come up in the youth hockey programs, as my own kids did from the age of five. Games on the pond don't have any rules, and we had two rocks at either end of the ice surface to serve as goals. When I got to the ninth grade, I started lifting weights, developed a lot of strength, and decided I'd try out for wrestling instead.

The two subjects I loved at school were science and history, and I had wonderful teachers in both. I was taught United States history by Bill Schenck, who lives in upstate New York now and must be eighty-something years old. He is a good Democrat, I might add, and he taught me well.

Many of my favorite childhood memories are centered around the time we spent as a family on Long Island. Eastern Long Island is exquisitely beautiful on clear blue summer days, but I always loved being there in the winter when it wasn't quite so crowded. There is an extraordinary landscape that melts into the seascape; it is bleak in a very beautiful way.

I will always feel connected to the sea. Even though I love Vermont and have lived there most of my adult life, every time I go to East Hampton, I smell the ocean, and I feel like I'm home again. My childhood in Long Island made Vermont a natural fit for me. At heart, I'm a country person.

CHAPTER

★ 2 ★

M y father had what can best be described as an enormous personality. He was incredibly charismatic and also incredibly strong-minded. As they say in politics, he could suck all the oxygen out of a room. He and I had as complicated a relationship as he had with his own father, another magnetic and well-regarded individual who was a hard act to follow.

When he was seventeen, my father went to Yale. He had a great time, flunked freshman chemistry twice, and never graduated. He used to enjoy telling the story of how he got a 55 in chemistry, which meant he had to repeat his freshman year. The next year, he got a 50; his Yale career was over. The Second World War intervened, and he never went back to college.

Because he'd had diphtheria when he was a child and

had a tracheostomy for a long time, my father couldn't join the army. Instead, he went to work for Pan American, running freight operations supplying Allied troops in North Africa and spending a lot of time in places like Nigeria and the Sudan. He then worked in India as a logistics manager helping to resupply the Chinese nationalists who were holding out against Japan. After the Japanese cut the Burma Road, the only way to get material to the nationalists was by air. This was called "flying the hump," the "hump" being the Himalayas. Later, my father went to China, working with Chinese nationalists against the Communists as they were conquering the country.

In 1946, Dad came back to the States; my grandfather was very sick and died in 1950. Suddenly, my father had to make some money. He was twenty-seven and married with one child—me—and another one on the way. He felt an enormous amount of responsibility for us, his own mother, and his sisters.

My parents encouraged me to get out of the house at a relatively early age. In the summers, this meant getting a job. My first summer job was as a counselor at a sailing camp at age fourteen. I was paid in French fries and hamburgers.

When I was sixteen, I worked with two other teenagers on the Big B cattle ranch near Belle Glade, Florida, which is a town eighty miles northwest of Miami on the southeast shore of Lake Okeechobee. We were two sixteen-year-olds and a fifteen-year-old out on our own in the world, for the summer at least. The three of us lived in a little apartment above the ranch office, and we worked ten hours a day, six and a half days a week, earning $1.15 an hour for the first six days and $1.25 on Sunday—at that time, Florida agricultural minimum wage.

Most of the time, we worked clearing land for the cattle ranch. On Sundays, our job was to spot the planes that were dusting crops or killing weeds. We'd stand on either end of a field holding poles to guide the prop plane as it swooped down and sprayed. I remember feeling the cool mist of the herbicide on my bare chest as the plane went over. At the time, we thought nothing of it.

Everybody else working the ranch was Cuban. Castro had nationalized the ranches in Cuba, and these workers had come to America, dropping down a notch in status in the process. The owner of a ranch in Cuba was the manager of the ranch in Florida, the forklift operator in Florida had been the manager in Cuba, and the ranch hand in Florida had been the forklift operator in Cuba. The manager was the only one who spoke any English, so we learned to speak some Spanish (a lot of which could not be repeated in polite company, as I learned a little too late).

Another year, I worked in the back office of a brokerage house on Wall Street. In the summer, the family moved out to Long Island while my father stayed in the city to work. When we got to be old enough, each of the Dean boys worked summers in the city and lived with my father. He liked having us around. In those days, the financial services industry was not yet computerized, and my brothers and I helped keep track of the voluminous paper records.

When I graduated from high school, my father wanted me to take an extra year before I went to college, as he wished he had done himself. I followed his advice and got an English-Speaking Union scholarship to a boys' boarding school in England.

It was a great experience, but I found the restrictive reputation of English public schools to be well earned. I enjoyed the English dry sense of humor, but a British public school is pretty cruel and the rules are strict. When I was in England, I played rugby and basketball. At home, I was by no means a good basketball player, but in the land of "football" and cricket, I was Jerry West *and* Pete Maravich.

This time abroad did give me the opportunity to travel, which I've never forgotten. I went to Tunisia for Christmas, and visited Corsica and Sardinia. A group of us drove in a Land Rover to Istanbul through Bulgaria and Yugoslavia in the spring of 1967.

To go off on my own for thirteen months at age seventeen was an eye-opening experience, and I thank my parents and the English-Speaking Union for it.

When it came time to choose a college, I looked to my father. Despite never graduating, he'd had a great time at Yale. Rather than send me on the official tour, my father took me on a tour of his own. His version featured such highlights as "Here's where I rolled a shot put down the hall and knocked down the dean's piano." I later found out that he would have preferred for me to go to Williams College, but his stories made Yale irresistible.

CHAPTER

★ 3 ★

When I graduated from high school in 1966, the phenomenon of the sixties was still isolated in places like Berkeley, where the free speech movement had been under way for several years. But when I came back from England in the fall of '67, the sixties were in full swing. George W. Bush graduated in '68; his senior year was my freshman year. The gulf between our experiences was much larger, though; it was as if we were a generation apart.

Yale was undergoing dramatic changes. Under its pioneering dean of admissions R. Inslee Clark, the school was taking many more students from diverse backgrounds. The unofficial quota system for Jewish students was discontinued; more students were recruited from public schools. In 1969, women were admitted.

Kingman Brewster was the Yale University president who appointed Clark. Brewster was an extraordinarily deft president. He backed Clark in the face of alumni outrage over his curtailing of legacy admissions. He was also the only Ivy League president who kept his job in the late '60s and early '70s. Yale was relatively riot free, a testimony to Brewster's diplomatic skills. He ended up as the ambassador to the Court of St. James's (i.e., to the United Kingdom), which I think was very appropriate.

The new admissions policy helped make Yale into a great institution. It is one of the preeminent intellectual centers of America and not just because it provides an excellent education. There were probably twenty schools that were equally outstanding in the sixties but Yale became deeply committed to diversity and egalitarianism in a way that many other places were not at that time. I was profoundly influenced by the new environment.

My major at Yale was political science; I chose it mainly because I had some advance placements and didn't need to sit through any introductory courses. I was lucky enough to be taught by some remarkable professors. I took an international relations course taught by William Foltz, who is still on the faculty as professor of African studies and political science, and who began my lifelong interest in international relations.

The Polish-born writer Jerzy Kosinski, the author of *The Painted Bird* and *Being There*, was one of my more unusual and extraordinary teachers. I remember his dry and biting sense of humor and also his piercing eyes. I took a lecture course and seminar from the controversial, and brilliant, law professor Charlie Reich who published *The Greening of America* in 1970. Yale had possibly the finest history department in America when I was there. I was taught by John Morton Blum, Robin Winks, and Gaddis Smith, all prominent historians. C. Vann Woodward was on the faculty as well.

Two of my political science professors had personal experience with the Eastern bloc. Frederick Barghoorn had been arrested and held as a spy by the Soviet authorities in Moscow in 1963, and Wolfgang Leonhard had been a Communist Party official in East Germany before defecting to the West. He was a very charismatic lecturer. Thirty-five years later, I can still hear Leonhard's voice saying: *"Pravda lies in such a way that not even the opposite is so."*

Yale was a place of brilliance at the center of intellectual ferment. I wasn't ready to be a serious student, as my transcripts demonstrated. But I rarely missed a class, and my course load was more than what was required. When I achieved honors, it was because I loved the course and was willing to put in the time.

I had two African-American roommates my freshman year: Don Roman from Memphis, Tennessee, and Ralph Dawson from South Carolina. Each was one of the finest students in his segregated high school. Our fourth roommate was Joe Mancini, who was from rural Pennsylvania.

We'd play cards—bid whist usually. I'd go to bed first, at

eleven or twelve, because I had an eight o'clock Spanish class. They'd keep playing and Ralph would go to bed at two or three. Don would then give up and crash at four. I'd wake up in the morning to go to my Spanish class, and Joe would be finishing up a hand of solitaire.

Ralph was a very charismatic young man, and he ended up as chairman of the black students' alliance. There were perhaps forty black men in a class of a thousand, and our room became a center for the black students.

Today Ralph Dawson works for a major law firm in New York City as a labor lawyer, and Don Roman is a very successful estate planner in Atlanta. Joe Mancini dropped out after his freshman year, but later got his degree and is now a successful lawyer in Florida. We had a reunion in Atlanta in September 2003, the first time I'd seen Joe in twenty-five years.

When I was at Yale, the political discourse was dominated by ideas from the left. I was situated then where I've been ever since, in the center. I didn't support the Vietnam War, but I certainly wasn't a member of the Students for a Democratic Society, the radical movement that occupied the president's office at Columbia in 1968 and spawned the Weathermen.

I have always felt comfortable in the middle; it's where most reasonable solutions are found. One of the most troubling things about the Bush administration is its substitution of ideology for thought. In pursuit of dogmatic rigor, people are ignored. The far left was guilty of this during the sixties. Now the far right, through the Bush administration, seeks to impose its vision on a middle-of-the-road America.

I was a junior in college when the draft was instituted. I remember that I got number 143, which meant I would have most likely been sent to Vietnam had I passed the physical. I went to Fort Hamilton in Brooklyn for my exam; there were people of all shapes, sizes, colors, and dispositions, each standing around wearing nothing but their undershorts.

In my junior year of high school, when I was running track, I began to develop back pain. It got to the point where I couldn't run. Once in a while, after playing football, I couldn't straighten up from my stance. I eventually went to an orthopedic surgeon, who told me I had a spondylosis —an unfused vertebra—in my back. My father introduced me to a young man who'd undergone surgery to try to correct the condition; he was out of commission for six months after the operation. It sounded like a horrible procedure, so I decided not to have the surgery.

Nowadays I lead a vigorous outdoor life, but I still get pain in my back and in my legs, particularly the left one. When I try walking after I've been sitting still, I'll limp the first fifty yards or so. I can't run much, except over short distances in airports.

My back condition meant that I was given a 1Y classification by the army. I could be drafted only in a time of national emergency, I suspect. The army didn't want to have someone like me on their disability rolls. If I'd been drafted, I'd have gone to Vietnam, even though I was against the war. As it turned out, the war was to have a profound effect on my family.

CHAPTER

★ 4 ★

It seemed that all my friends were choosing to go to law school after they graduated from Yale. I chose Colorado instead. The summer after my sophomore year, I'd lived in Denver moving furniture, and I loved the place. At that time, I thought it didn't matter what work you did, as long as you were happy where you lived.

I ended up with a job pouring concrete. One of the guys in the foundation company was a young man from New Mexico called T.J. He was much older than I was, at least twenty-five or twenty-six. After the company went under, he started in business for himself and he hired me. Pouring concrete was very hard work. My job was to oil heavy metal forms and assemble them in a giant jigsaw puzzle and tie rebar into the spaces between the forms. Then I bent the rebar and poured in the concrete over the top. After the concrete had hardened for a couple of days, the forms were taken down. I had also landed a job working the night shift washing dishes in a restaurant, so I was working sixteen-hour days.

I lived way up in a cabin in the mountains in a little place called Ashcroft, an old silver mining town about ten miles from Aspen. I came down the mountain only to work and ski. I skied for eighty days. I'd get up, ski all day, and go to work at four. All I did was work and ski, which was fine for a while because, Vermont aside, Colorado has the greatest skiing in the world.

Outwardly, my family was fairly understanding about what I was doing. It was usually easy to figure when my father disapproved of something, because he would descend into silences that were positively deafening. He was clearly disappointed when I left Yale and didn't find a "real job."

My sojourn in the mountains taught me one thing: I wasn't cut out for a life in a resort community. After a visit with my brother Charlie in North Carolina, I planned to go to Bogotá, Colombia, where some friends were teaching English at a school. I missed the plane. I've taken many hundreds of flights in my life, and this is the only time that's ever happened. I realized that there was a reason I missed the plane. I cut short my intended trip, went home, and decided to get to work.

I thought I had a few options open to me, and one was teaching. While I was at Yale, I'd taught seventh- and eighth-grade social studies for three months in a middle school in New Haven. The experience gave me an enormous respect for teachers. Until you have actually tried to teach social studies to sometimes indifferent eighth-grade students, you have no idea how hard it is. You're on your feet performing in front of a class for hours on end, and as soon as one group of kids leaves the room, another is filing in. You can't even go to the bathroom. The teacher has to impose some measure of discipline while trying to impart knowledge at the same time, and the lessons have to be prepared every day.

I was also considering careers in either medicine or finance. I'd always liked science, and I had a notion that being a doctor would be something I might enjoy. However, that would mean going back to school, since I hadn't taken any science courses when I was in college. I was in no way prepared to go to medical school. The country was in the midst of a recession, and there was a tremendous demand for professional qualifications and the security they offered. Law school and medical school were both very competitive. Wall Street offered itself as the path of least resistance.

In September 1972, I went to work at a firm called Clark, Dodge & Co. As a trainee, I was assigned to a trucking and railroads analyst, so I learned a lot about . . . trucking and railroads. Later, I trained to be a salesperson—a broker. I discovered I wasn't a particularly good broker. My problem was that I didn't like calling people to advise them to move a stock unless I knew something about it and actually thought they should sell. I was as careful with other people's money as I was with my own. As a result, my commissions were never very impressive.

The part of the financial industry I did like was money management. I became an assistant to the president of a small mutual fund, a man named Bob Hill. Bob and his other assistant, Mary Wong, and I ran the fund among us. Because there were only the three of us, I learned a lot about the stock market in particular, and about finance in general. These lessons were useful later on when I became governor.

I came to realize, however, that I didn't want to live in New York. It's the most exciting place on earth, but for me, a few days is enough. If you want to work all the time, New York is the most convenient city there is. But I missed outdoor life every day.

I wasn't concerned that I might be passing up a lucrative career. For me, life has never been about money. That's partly because I've always had enough to get by. I know this sounds insincere for a politician to say, but what has motivated me more than money has been the urge to make the world a better place. I knew from my experience of teaching that I wasn't cut out to try to save the world in a classroom.

When I taught in New Haven, the social issues the kids were facing seemed overwhelming to me. I knew I couldn't meet all of their needs, and that constantly frustrated me. There were twenty-five or thirty kids in a class, and while you might identify the problems, you didn't have time to address them properly.

I had a friend in New York who had been in the same situation I was in—she'd graduated from Yale and decided later to pursue a career in medicine, so she went back to school and completed the science courses she needed. Her experience showed me that it could be done.

In the fall of 1973, I took a tentative first step in my medical career. Going to medical school was a significant commitment of money and time, and I wanted to make sure I was making the right decision, so I volunteered to work in the emergency room at St. Vincent's Hospital in New York City.

The ER was small and cramped and always busy on Monday nights when I worked. We were so short-staffed, I was given some responsibilities in spite of my lack of schooling; on top of the more menial jobs like running blood up to the lab, I ended up taking blood pressures and temperatures as well.

I loved the ER. The experience convinced me I wanted to be a physician. If I went into medicine today, I'd be an emergency room doctor. I loved the fast pace and variety of work.

The next step was to complete my science requirements. I decided I'd try the biology course at the Columbia School of General Studies. My mother had beaten that particular path for me. After her boys were all out of the house, she went back to school at Columbia General Studies and got her degree in art history. In her forties, she went on to start her own art appraisal business and is still running it today at seventy-four.

One day I got on the subway and went uptown to register for biology. As I registered, I heard a very familiar voice. "Howard," said my mother, "what are you doing here?"

I asked, "What are *you* doing here?"

She told me she was doing some volunteer work. I explained what I was up to and pleaded with my mother not to give away my secret. I wanted to see if I could put my toe back in the academic water first before breaking the news of a career change to my father. "Whatever you do," I implored, "you have to promise not to tell Dad."

I started out taking freshman biology. I'd been out of school for three years, and I had no idea if I could get back into the rigors of study. I knew I'd be studying with a lot of smart and aggressive people who were determined to go to medical school. I took the course and I did well. I reached a point of no return. If I was going to get my science requirements, there was no way I was going to endure three years of night school; I was going to have to give up work and study full-time, which meant a conversation with my father.

To break the news, I took him out to dinner. It was clearly an unusual occasion, since I was paying and my mother wasn't invited. I told him I was going to quit work, move back home, and study to go to medical school.

Years later, my father told me he thought I was nuts at the time. He couldn't understand why I would throw away a career on Wall Street to go to medical school. He kept his feelings to himself for a long time; I was probably already governor before he said anything. It took great self-control on his part to curb his instinct to speak out. I've always been grateful for that.

My father was very clear about his wishes, but for the good of the family he sometimes went along with a course of action he might not necessarily have agreed with. This is one of the reasons I admired him. He knew it would be devastating if he said he thought I was wasting my time. My guess is, I would have done it anyway, but his disapproval would have made my life a lot harder. He had the wisdom to let me make my own way, and he had the self-discipline to allow me to take the chance that I would fail. He knew I had to make my own mistakes.

CHAPTER

★ 5 ★

I moved back in with my parents, returning to the room I'd lived in as a child. I put my nose to the grindstone and worked. I had never worked particularly hard at Yale and it hadn't made me happy. I realized there was a simple cause and effect: If I'm directionless and coasting, I'm not happy. I didn't really get to be a happy person until I went to medical school. I knew when I was taking my night school courses that I was on the right track. I took organic chemistry, calculus, chemistry, biology, and biochemistry in a year, and I loved it.

When it came time to interview for medical school, there were three places I looked at seriously. One was New York Medical College, where my uncle was a physician. Another was the Albert Einstein College of Medicine in the Bronx, which is part of Yeshiva University. The last was

Columbia Presbyterian. I got into New York Medical College and Einstein, and I was wait-listed at Columbia.

My uncle Bill Felch at New York Medical College was very helpful to me even though I didn't end up going to his school. He had done an internship at Columbia Presbyterian in the forties, when you had to live in the hospital full-time. He helped me think through the decision to go to medical school, and I was thankful to have him as a role model.

I made my decision when I went for my interview at Einstein. I met with a surgeon named Dr. Anderson, with whom I felt tremendous chemistry during the interview. Dr. Anderson had a no-nonsense air about him. I think he was impressed that I was performing so well at Columbia after I'd goofed off academically during college. He wrote, I later found out, a remarkable recommendation, which I'm sure made the difference.

I knew I would get in when I finished the interview. What's more, I knew Einstein was where I ought to go. Another, more concrete factor was that the school offered a three-year program rather than the usual four-year stretch. I was twenty-five years old and eager to practice.

At Einstein, I became active in university politics. I led a movement to get students on the admissions committee. Together with a great friend named Lee Kaplan, who's at Massachusetts General Hospital now, I wrote a guidebook for students. It wasn't just the usual information about how to rent apartments and where to get the best pizza, but how to deal with the academic bureaucracy.

The most important event that happened to me at

Einstein was meeting Judy Steinberg. I knew Judy because we would occasionally both do the *New York Times* crossword puzzle in the more tedious classes. Judy and I were both coming off relationships, and Judy was missing her college friends. She had said to herself that she'd go to the next social event that presented itself. For my part, I thought Judy was just adorable, and I was determined to ask her out. So one Friday afternoon I saw her in the library and asked her to dinner.

Coming from Wall Street, I was used to wearing a tie every day. I even carried a briefcase at medical school, which Judy thought was unusual. She was more of a blue-jeans-and-sweater person. She saw me and thought "Oh Lord but what the heck," and she said yes.

We had our first date in my parents' apartment. I invited three other friends. I dressed casually, for me, in khakis and a dress shirt. Of course my friends turned up in sandals, T-shirts, and shorts. It was a big spaghetti dinner. Richard Willing, now a prominent journalist, who is very entertaining, told an outrageous story. As he unraveled the tale, I thought to myself, "If she laughs, we're in; if she doesn't, this relationship is over before it's begun."

Richard got to the end of the story, and Judy turned red but laughed like crazy. I saw that she had a terrific sense of humor, even though she would never have used the kind of language Willing indulged in. Much later I found out that Judy left the dinner thinking, "He's a nice guy, but I like his friends better than I like him." Fortunately, Judy's patient, and I had time to grow on her.

On another occasion I had dinner at her apartment.

Judy decided she was going to cook hamburgers for me. Judy had seen a Craig Claiborne recipe for hamburgers in *The New York Times*. The recipe called for laying a bed of salt in a frying pan, heating the heck out of it, and cooking the hamburger on top. Judy had tried the recipe one night using the little bit of salt it specified, and the hamburger turned out juicy and delicious. If a little bit of salt worked well, Judy reasoned, a lot of salt would be even better. That was what she tried when I came over. Of course, the hamburger sucked it all up and she served what was basically a cake of salt. A saltburger. Judy, who is an extremely polite person, took one bite and spat it out, but I ate the whole thing—and had eight glasses of water on the side.

Judy and I have been married twenty-two years, and we really are life partners. Judy says I'm still the same person she met almost thirty years ago. After liking my friends better, Judy says she came to appreciate the way I'd see the good in each person, enjoy them, and treat them with respect. She liked the fact that I was interested in things and always wanted to know more, and that with me you never have to guess what I'm thinking. I hope at least some of these things are true.

Judy had gone to medical school by way of Princeton. Over time, of course, I got to know her family and she got to know mine. Judy's father, Herman, is a well-known gastroenterologist in New York City, and I admire him a great deal. Herman's parents emigrated from Poland and Russia in the early 1900s, his mother sailing to America at age seventeen without the approval of her family.

Judy's grandparents eventually ran a pharmacy in East

New York, and her father used to sneak into Ebbett's Field when he was a kid to watch the Brooklyn Dodgers. He went to a very good New York high school, and he could have gone to City College in New York, which was free, but he was also accepted by Columbia, which wasn't. His immigrant Jewish family scraped together everything they had to send him to Columbia.

For four years Herman rode two hours every day on the subway to go to Columbia, with a bag lunch in his lap on the way out. He loved books, but he couldn't afford to buy them and never owned a book the whole time he was at college. That used to make my kids' heads spin. One of his professors would open up his library to students, who could borrow any book for as long as they needed it.

Medical school was a lot of hard work, but it didn't seem like hard work at the time. I loved being on the wards. Because I was on the three-year track, there were no breaks during the year.

Of course, I had a lot to learn. On one occasion, in a psychiatric hospital in the Bronx, I was locked in a secure ward with a patient. I asked him, "Can you tell me, sir, why you're here?"

He said, "I don't know, man. I think I killed somebody."

I was terrified. I'd heard the key turn in the heavy metal door, so I thought I was in a locked room with a murderer. It turned out he had lost a child to what we would now call SIDS. He blamed himself and had spiraled into a horrible depression.

I learned the first half of a valuable lesson when I was a medical student in a Bronx hospital. I was in the emergency room, and the first patient I saw was a young African-American girl of about thirteen, who was pregnant. Her mother was with her, and when I told the girl she was pregnant, her mother was furious. Three or four years later, I was doing my first emergency room rotation in a hospital in Vermont, and a young white girl came in. She was also about thirteen. She also turned out to be pregnant, and sure enough, her mother was furious. There is a myth that social problems are the province of minorities in this country. The truth is, the incidence of teenage pregnancy and other social problems is higher among people who are poor, no matter what color they are.

In the last year of medical school, students choose the specialty they will pursue during their residency. The residency is a training program at a hospital that usually runs three to five years, depending on the specialty. When students apply for a residency, they list their top ten schools, and the schools list their top several hundred choices for residents. All of the choices go into a computer, and the computer cross-matches the students and the schools. I got sent to Vermont.

I didn't get into any of my top three choices. My fourth choice was the ambulatory care program at the University of Vermont. I'd been visiting the state since 1966, including trips to see my brother Bill, who graduated from the University of Vermont in Burlington in 1977. Some really close friends had a farmhouse at Bondville, at the foot of Stratton Mountain, and I had gone up there to spend time in the summer.

To me, the secret of Vermont is the summer. I love skiing, but when I started visiting Vermont in the summer, I found the place to be absolutely magical. Like a lot of places that have long, cold winters, Vermont has a spectacular summer. The country is lush and green, the streams are bubbling, and the days are long and lazy. Soon after I left New York, I realized it was just what I wanted. Judy was going through the four-year program at Einstein, so, alone, I moved to Burlington in May 1978.

CHAPTER

★ 6 ★

For any doctor, the first year of the residency—the internship—is without question the most miserable year of your working life. There are 168 hours in a week, and it was not unusual for an intern to work 100 of them. I had little time for much of anything else, other than sleep. Once when Judy came up to visit, she opened the icebox and found nothing in it but a five-pound jar of peanut butter and a loaf of bread. When Judy graduated in 1979, she came up to join me in Burlington. We got married in January 1981.

After we got married, I quit drinking. When I drank, I would drink a lot and do outrageous things, and then I wouldn't drink again for a while. I realized that what was very funny when you're eighteen is not very funny when you're thirty. I had a terrible hangover after my bachelor party, which didn't help. So I quit. Drinking served no useful purpose in my life, and I just got tired of it. I haven't had a drink in over twenty-two years.

When we got married, Judy was still working on her residency. She then started a hematology fellowship at McGill University in Montreal. We had a commuter marriage for a year. I was on call one out of every three weekends, and Judy was on call one out of every three weekends, so when one of us was off, we'd travel to see the other. I hated having a commuter marriage, and I wouldn't do it again. Finally, she moved back to Burlington and later joined me in a medical practice.

Judy and I worked in Shelburne, just to the south of Burlington, and most of our patients were suburban families. Shelburne was a town in transition, fast becoming a bedroom community for Burlington; there were engineers and lawyers together with farmers. We were internists, not family practitioners, so we didn't provide pediatric services for very young children; we treated people from 5 to 105. We made house calls then, and Judy continues to do so.

Judy and I have different styles when it comes to practicing medicine. Judy is very methodical; she goes by the book. She'll look at a patient's symptoms and signs, look at all possible differential diagnoses, and, step-by-step, plan out what she needs to do. I am more apt to jump straight to the conclusion based on my observation of the facts. Both styles can work, and we complement each other very well.

• • •

I had always liked President Carter. I thought he was a decent, honest person. He was the first president to systematically link human rights and foreign policy, and that resonated with me. I also liked the fact that he was a scientist (he'd done graduate work in nuclear physics). He would approach a problem rationally, and facts mattered a lot to him. The worldview I gained at college, together with the practical, empirical work that a doctor is involved in, seemed to be represented politically in Jimmy Carter.

In December 1979, I was reading an article in the local paper about the Carter reelection campaign being kicked off. The person who was running the campaign locally was a state senator named Esther Sorrell, who lived, it turned out, five doors down from our apartment. It was Esther who got me involved in politics in Vermont.

Of all the Dean boys, my brother Charlie had been the first to get involved in party politics, doing some work for the McGovern campaign in North Carolina in 1972. Both of us were confirmed Democrats by that stage, much to the consternation of our father, who resolutely remained a Republican.

My father's politics were mainly determined by his attitude toward money. More than anything, he was a fiscal conservative, which wasn't incompatible with being a Republican forty years ago. My father was not particularly liberal about social issues, but he wasn't particularly conservative, either. Today he would be considered a moderate business-oriented Republican; he wanted the budget run properly. In that way, I am very much my father's son.

I had my first taste of politics in 1964 at age fifteen. I

spent three weeks in California with a friend whose father got us tickets to the Republican convention in San Francisco. During the convention, Nelson Rockefeller was famously booed off the stage, marking the ascension of the right wing of the party. I had no idea of the significance of what was happening. Because my father liked him, I was for Barry Goldwater, who won the nomination. My much more sophisticated friends were for Governor William Scranton of Pennsylvania, and a couple even admitted to liking Lyndon Johnson, although no one at my school would have dared call themselves a Democrat.

At the convention in 1964, I didn't feel much of a thrill at all of the razzmatazz that surrounds these events. The showbiz of politics has never been particularly interesting to me. Still, I enjoyed seeing the famous people. We rushed up to the Fairmont Hotel, where the Republicans had their headquarters, to see who was coming and going.

My first involvement in Vermont politics was strictly local: I helped start up the Citizens' Waterfront Group with Rick Sharp, an attorney, and Tom Hudspeth, an environmental professor at the University of Vermont. There was an abandoned railway line that ran along the waterfront in Burlington. A plan existed to develop part of the land, but we wanted public access to the water, which was to be secured with a nine-mile bike path along the shore of Lake Champlain.

It was a grassroots effort: A few hundred members in our group applied pressure to two successive mayoral administrations. In the end, we won. The bike path was built, and the waterfront is now one of Burlington's treasures. A jazz festival is held there every year, and eighty thousand people come to watch fireworks on July 4. Through the Citizens' Waterfront Group, I got to know people in local politics. It's one of the most important projects I've ever been involved in; it changed the face of the largest city in the state and made a public resource available to residents and tourists alike.

We carried the ideals behind the Citizens' Waterfront Group into other communities after I became governor. We made sure that farms and unspoiled areas in the state will never be developed, and we set aside hundreds and thousands of acres of shorefront and forests, which will always be accessible to the public.

After I read the story about the Carter campaign, I went to Esther Sorrell's house to introduce myself. Though she was thirty years older than I, we became good friends. Esther, her sister Peggy, and their friend Maureen McNamara used to meet every Friday and watch *Vermont This Week*, the local equivalent of *Washington Week*. I'd join the three of them. We'd eat the cookies they baked, watch the show, and talk politics. I received a thorough education in Vermont politics in the process.

It turned out I'd already met another sister, Audrey. When I first moved up to Burlington, I went to register to vote, and it was Audrey I saw. When I registered, I was an intern and I didn't have any time to do anything other than sign my name. But by December 1979, I was in my second year of residency. I worked a lot with Esther, licking envelopes and that kind of thing. We wanted to win the Vermont primary to offset Massachusetts, Ted Kennedy's home state. That's exactly what happened.

Afterward, Esther asked me if I'd be one of Vermont's representatives at the convention. "Why don't you run for national delegate?" she said.

I replied, "I can't do that; I don't know anybody. I've only been in the state for two years."

She said, "The kind of people who get to be national delegates are former governors and high-ranking people who haven't done anything like the work you've done. I think you should do it."

I repeated, "I don't know anybody," and she said, "Well, *we* do."

So Peggy and Esther opened their Rolodexes, and I made a couple hundred phone calls. I would say that Peg Hartigan or Esther Sorrell had asked me to call and would you kindly support me for national delegate? I came in third after the lieutenant governor and after Esther herself. Being elected a national delegate helped me get started in Vermont. I owe a tremendous debt to Esther and Peggy as a result. I could never have done anything around the state without them. They knew everybody and introduced me to all of them. I think they also helped mold my politics. They were old-time ethnic Democrats who didn't come from an elite background. They shaped me into a pragmatic Democrat. I was friendly with the younger, more liberal Democrats because they were my age, but I didn't vote with them. I didn't relate to their political sensibilities.

Esther Sorrell was truly the mother of the Democratic

Party in Vermont. The party had a somewhat anemic history in the state—there were no Democratic governors from 1853 to 1962. In 1958, Congressman William Meyer was the first Democrat Vermont sent to Washington. He lasted one term. (Pat Leahy, in 1974, was elected Vermont's first Democratic senator.) But there was nothing anemic about Esther. In 1958, the governor's race was very close, and the Democrats lost only after a recount. The county chairman called in Esther and a group of women who'd worked on the campaign and said, "Girls, you worked really hard. How about we give you a party?"

And Esther said, "How about you give us some seats on the county committee?"—which at that time was an all-male group.

Esther was a state senator for ten years. She once made a speech on Good Friday in favor of increasing the pathetic amount of money people on public assistance received. Her speech was so good that she actually changed some people's minds, and the measure passed; it is a speech people still talk about to this day.

I went to the 1980 convention in New York City, where Ted Kennedy was pitted against Jimmy Carter. I would vote with the Carter people, who were thirty years older than I was, and then I'd go out at night with the Kennedy people, who were my age. I got to be friends with both sides.

When I came back from the convention, Mark Kaplan, the state chair, called me and said he wanted me to be the chair of Chittenden County, the largest county in the state. The incumbent was very ill and had to step down. I tried to say no, but Kaplan said I was apparently the only person who could get along with both the Carter people and the Kennedy people, who comprised the two factions in the county. He said I had to do it, so I did.

As chair of the largest county, I started to get some notice. My job was to try to get Democrats elected to the state senate. After I had been doing that for two years, I decided to run for the state legislature. Someone who represented my district had decided to run for the senate, so I ran for the house seat she was vacating. The district was in Burlington, and it was the most liberal, working-class district in the state. I was running against a progressive. Bernie Sanders had won the mayor's race in Burlington in 1981 by ten votes, beating the five-term Democrat incumbent. There was a very strong Progressive Party in the ward and no Republican Party whatsoever. So, interestingly, I ended up running against a candidate to my left in my first election.

I was living in a little apartment in the North End of town. Every day I'd leave work and drive directly to the ward to knock on doors. I knew if I went home first I'd find all sorts of reasons not to go back and pound the pavement. You've got to screw up your courage to go and knock on strangers' doors. Every day I'd bang on a hundred doors. I knocked on every door in the ward twice over the summer and fall. One woman answered the door and said, "You must really want this."

"Yes, I do," I replied.

There was a wonderful woman in her mid-eighties named Fanny Gardner who was single and had lived alone all her life. She had a coal heater in her house, and she'd go down into the basement and dig out the coal to put in her stove. She loved to talk—really talk—and I got to know her fairly well. My opponent was a good guy, but we made sure Fanny was available when he was out knocking on doors in the neighborhood. She kept him busy for three hours at a time.

I won the election. It was 1982, and I had secured my first elective office.

CHAPTER

★ **7** ★

The Vermont House was a great education for me.
When I came in. I was a member of the minority
party, and I served on the Education Committee,
which was chaired by a liberal Democrat named Marie
Condon. This was my first experience in elected office, and
Marie taught me a lot. For one thing, she showed me how
counterproductive thoughts of revenge and vindictiveness
can be. Someone had gotten my blood boiling, and I must
have said I was going to retaliate. Marie took me aside
and said, "You're going to do really well here, but you've got
to get over this chip on your shoulder that tells you to fix
somebody's wagon if they cross you."

After two years in the house, I announced that I was
going to run for the job of minority whip. This was unusual,
as the post wasn't vacant; I was trying to unseat the incum-

bent. I was a member of a group of young legislators who called themselves the Blue Shirts. We were moderate Republicans and moderate and liberal Democrats. I wanted to represent the Blue Shirts and try to make my way into the leadership.

I got the job without there even having to be a vote. The minority whip became minority leader, and I took his old job. The vote, had it ever come to pass, would have been extremely interesting. There were 72 Democrats, and based on what I had been promised, I thought I'd win 38–34. My opponent thought *he* was going to win 42–30. My 38 commitments and his 42 added up to 80, which meant 8 of our colleagues had lied to us. We never compared notes, but we both had a pretty good idea of who had said what to whom.

The Vermont House sits for about four and a half months a year. For those months, I would commute the forty miles from Burlington to Montpelier. The house didn't meet on Mondays and we ended our session at noon on Friday, so I'd work on Mondays and Friday afternoons in the doctor's office, in addition to Tuesday, Wednesday, and Thursday evenings.

In Vermont, state representative and lieutenant governor are both part-time jobs. I practiced as a doctor until the day I became governor. This system works out well, because if you pass some impractical law and then you have to go back to work and fill out all the forms to comply with it, you'll think twice before doing it again.

In 1986, when I was in my second term in the legislature, I decided to run for lieutenant governor. (This is possible in

Vermont; the lieutenant governor and the governor are elected on separate tickets.) Judy and I were living in the same apartment in Burlington's North End that I'd had when I was an intern. When Judy became pregnant for the second time, we didn't have room for two kids in the apartment, so we moved to the house we live in today, which meant I left my district—which meant I couldn't run for my house seat again. I had to choose between running for the state senate, running for lieutenant governor, and running for the U.S. Congress. Running for Congress against Jim Jeffords would have been an impossible task. Vermont has only one U.S. representative, and Jim Jeffords had represented the state since 1974. Jeffords was an icon even at that time.

I decided in the end that running for lieutenant governor was a better idea than running for the state senate. A state senate race in the largest county in the state is extremely difficult. I concluded a statewide race was not much more difficult, so I ran for lieutenant governor.

I went to see the Republican lieutenant governor, a very decent guy named Peter Smith, who later became Vermont's congressman. I told him I was going to run against him. He laughed at me, saying, "Okay, but I'm going to kick your butt."

I said, "Maybe you will, but I'm going to run against you anyway." This was all said very good-naturedly.

A week later, Peter Smith announced he was running for governor. He must have known he was going to run when I went to see him, but he didn't mention it. Now I was running for an open seat.

What ensued was the hardest race I ever had in many ways, although it was far from the ugliest. I ran against Susan Auld, the majority leader in the house. It was neck and neck with two or three weeks to go. Both of us worked our tails off. My brother Jim came up with his girlfriend, moved in, and ran my first statewide campaign. He did a great job, and I finally won by about nine points.

The lieutenant governor presides over the state senate. You have an office, and you have one staff person. In the course of working with the senate, the lieutenant governor learns written parliamentary procedure and the unwritten rules of how to get things done. Both these lessons would turn out to be very helpful when I was governor.

The lieutenant governor sits on a committee that gives everybody their committee assignments, so at least for the first few days of the session, everybody wants to be your friend. You also refer bills to committees, which gives you the power to decide the direction in which bills are going to go, because you know which committee is going to like which particular bill and which committee is going to have a problem with it. The lieutenant governorship is a great job. It's also a part-time job.

On the days I worked in the doctor's office, I never talked politics unless someone brought it up. A medical practitioner has a significant amount of power over his patients, and I didn't think it was appropriate to put on my lieutenant governor's hat. It would be like a barber discussing tax policy while he's giving you a shave; you're afraid that if you say the wrong thing, you're going to find half your ear missing.

In the doctor's office, I listened to people talk about their back pain or about their kids. They were worried about much more immediate and concrete concerns than most of what we talked about in the legislature. It was helpful to be reminded every day that the big fight you just had in the legislature over state aid to education had no meaning to the vast majority of voters.

In 1990, Esther Sorrell died after a long struggle with metastatic lung cancer. I remained close to the Sorrell family. Much later, when I was governor, I appointed Esther's son Bill state attorney general. The day Bill was sworn in as attorney general, I gave him a candle shaped like a donkey's head that his mother had given me years before. She'd told me to light it on a special occasion. Just before I left as governor, Bill gave me back the candle, which had remained unlit. Bill said we should save the candle so we could light it together one day and think of Esther.

Two days after Esther's death, Governor Madeline Kunin announced she wasn't going to run for reelection. There was a three-way struggle over who should run on the Democratic ticket, and I was one of the people involved. In the end, I thought it best that I not run for governor in 1990. I had two small children—Paul was four and Anne was five at the time. I also worried about the medical practice. I knew I couldn't run for governor and be a part-time physician. So we agreed that Peter Welch, who was president of the senate, would run. He ran a great race and lost by only six points to the Republican candidate, Richard Snelling.

Dick Snelling had been governor when I first got to the legislature. In 1984 he stepped down, and Madeline Kunin became the first female governor in Vermont history. In 1990, Snelling ran again and won. Governor Snelling and I had an interesting relationship. He didn't really think of me as a lieutenant governor; he thought of me more as a doctor and referred to me as such. He actually called me "Doctor." He assumed I knew everything about medicine but nothing about government.

When I first got to the legislature in 1983, I was the only doctor there. Snelling put together a health care package and asked me to cosponsor it. It was a well-put-together piece of legislation about controlling costs. I was a rookie legislator cosponsoring the governor's flagship bill alongside a senior Republican. The legislation was held up in committee by a very crusty conservative Republican named Madeline Harwood, and Governor Snelling had to water down the bill.

I was in the doctor's office after the day's legislative session ended, and the governor got me and his Republican sponsor on a conference call to tell us he was changing the bill to get it out of the committee. I said I would go along, but I was against the changes. He had a bunch of thirty-year-old staffers, all of whom are now prominent Republicans in Vermont. Snelling said, "We've thought about this a lot. This is what we're going to do and it makes sense." [*Pause for effect*] "Isn't that right, boys?" and we heard a chorus of "Yes, Governor" from around the office. Snelling was not one you disagreed with.

Once, the Democratic speaker had the House Appropriations Committee cut the salary of the only person who worked for me, Jane Williams. It was very painful for her— she had no other job. I went to the governor, and he saw the move for what it was. Snelling was great. He said it was ridiculous, it was an affront to the office, and he was going to see to it that the money was restored. The senate fixed it anyway, but I knew Governor Snelling meant what he said. This was a Republican governor talking to a man who could very well be his next opponent.

Dick Snelling was a person of integrity who wanted to run the government properly without regard to party, and I hope I've followed his example.

He had a great intellect. One of the state senators tells a story that late one night when the legislature was in session he was walking by the governor's office, and he saw Governor Snelling at his desk with his head down. The senator assumed the governor had nodded off, but when he looked more closely he saw that Snelling actually had his head in a book and was studying Sanskrit.

Snelling's daughter Diane is as smart as her father. After Dick's death, his wife, Barbara, became a state senator after serving as lieutenant governor. In 2002, she resigned due to poor health, and to fill her seat I appointed Diane. The right wing had by that time taken over the Chittenden County Republican apparatus, and they opposed the move. The Snellings had been responsible for a lot of the party's success, and this was a slap in their faces. It was a pleasure to ignore their protests as I appointed Dick's daughter to his wife's seat.

CHAPTER

★ 8 ★

On August 14, 1991, the phone rang in my doctor's office at eight o'clock in the morning. I was the only doctor working that day. Judy was getting ready to take the kids on vacation to her parents' house that night; I was due to work a few more days and then join them before we all visited my parents. Ted Fink, our partner, was already on vacation, although he hadn't yet left town, and I was covering for everyone.

I was conducting a physical examination when the call came in. It was very unusual to get interrupted during an exam, but I understood when the nurse told me the governor's office was on the line. You don't ask the governor if you can call back in ten minutes, so I asked my patient to excuse me for a second.

The call was from Bruce Post, one of Governor

Snelling's staffers. "I'm terribly sorry to inform you the governor's passed away," Bruce said. My first split-second reaction was that he was kidding, but I knew immediately by his tone of voice he wasn't. I then started to hyperventilate, which was something I'd never done in my entire life. I told myself to breathe normally because I wouldn't be of use to anyone if I kept that up.

Before doing anything else, I went back and finished the physical. I knew from experience that when something traumatic happens, getting to work helps me to bear down and think. More important, this was my responsibility as a doctor. I knew that the patient I was seeing wouldn't be able to get another appointment for quite some time, and I wanted to fulfill my commitment to him before beginning to assume the obligations of governorship.

Eventually, I was able to call Judy and tell her what happened. I then called Jane Williams, who was working in my office. Instead of heading straight to Montpelier, I sat for three hours in the doctor's office in Shelburne making phone calls. I stayed where I was because I had three phone lines in the doctor's office and only two at the lieutenant governor's. The state police arrived; the media showed up, and it was something of a circus. Of course, I wasn't interested in talking to the media; I was trying to ensure that authority would be transferred in an orderly manner.

Judy came in to see the rest of my morning's patients. At around 11:30, I went back to the house. The place was full of kids. A couple of college students were running a small playgroup out of our house for the summer. I took Anne and Paul aside and brought them into the bedroom. I told them what had happened and that I was going to be the governor. The kids both cried because I couldn't go on vacation with them. They were too young to understand what being governor meant.

Eventually, everybody got dressed up, and we all got in a car with a state police officer. I used to get driven by the governor's state police detail on the rare occasions the governor was out of state and I was acting governor. Now, of course, I was being driven to Montpelier to be sworn in as governor. Technically, I'd be acting governor until there was another election, and there was no legal requirement that I be sworn in at all. But I decided that I should have a swearing-in ceremony. I thought it would be symbolically important to the people of the state to see the formal transition.

I took the oath of office from the chief justice standing in the governor's office—now my office—with Judy and the kids. I rarely give written speeches, and usually I hate to do it. But on some very formal occasions, it's important that you have a prepared text. This was certainly one of those occasions. The important part of the speech said that we were going to move forward with Governor Snelling's economic recovery plan. I understood that Dick Snelling had been elected governor and not me, and it was up to me to continue to clean up the state's fiscal mess. The first piece of business would be improving the state's economic outlook.

The next few weeks were among the hardest of my life. I was a young governor, forty-one years old, and I had to succeed a man who was a giant both physically and intellectually, who had dominated the political scene in Vermont. The people of Vermont had no idea what to expect from me.

The 1991 recession was the worst in Vermont since the Depression. The slump was particularly hard in places like California and New England, which were heavily dependent on defense spending, which was being cut at the end of the Cold War. We'd lost 20 percent of all the manufacturing jobs in the state.

It had never crossed my mind that this might happen. I'd never given it a thought. People who knew Governor Snelling had said during the legislative session he didn't look well, but I never thought he seemed particularly ill, and he was only sixty-four years old. I was shocked to the core when Governor Snelling died.

No one is ever really prepared to be a chief executive until you become one. I had been at the center of politics in the state for ten years, but you don't know how the boss's shoes are going to fit until you have to step into them. The people's health care becomes your responsibility. The education of the children of the state is your responsibility. The responsibility might be shared, but as far as the people of Vermont were concerned, as the sign on Harry Truman's desk famously said, "The buck stops here."

When I first took office and someone shouted, "Governor!" I looked around to see who they were calling. I got some surprises those first few weeks. We set up a series of meetings with my predecessor's cabinet officials. Frank McDougall was Governor Snelling's secretary of commerce.

He was telling me about the job programs he was running, and at the end of the meeting, he mentioned, "Governor, what would you like me to do with the seventy-eight Abenaki Indian skeletons that I have in my closet?"

"What?"

Apparently, a house had been built on an Abenaki burial ground, and the skeletons had been unearthed. Via the University of Vermont, they'd ended up at the Department of Commerce and Community Affairs. Nobody knew what to do with them.

It took years to resolve that issue. We went back, bought the house that had been built on the burial ground, leveled it, and returned the bones to their proper and sacred resting place.

My part in the medical practice ended immediately. After I got in the car the morning Governor Snelling died, I never saw another patient. Judy and I talked about my trying to practice one day a week, but we concluded I couldn't do it. Since then, I haven't treated anyone formally, but I have had a few "Is there a doctor in the house?" experiences. I was giving an inaugural speech once and someone passed out. I immediately stopped speaking and went to help. The doctor in me reacted immediately; the politician in me was hoping my speech wasn't that uninspiring.

I do miss being a doctor. I miss interacting with my patients. Some of them even miss *me.* There's one elderly lady Judy sees who used to be my patient. Every time she sees Judy she gives her a kiss on the cheek to transmit to me. I miss the day-to-day interaction and the sense you get of what is important in your patients' lives.

• • •

The Vermont governor's office is on the fifth floor of the Pavilion Building on State Street in Montpelier. Dick Snelling had created a dark den in the office the first time he was governor. Madeline Kunin remade it so it was very light, and I grew to love the office. In 1938, Governor George Aiken described his office this way: "I look off to the east and see Mount Monadnock rearing its peak through the clouds. Tonight the lights of the neighbors' houses twinkle in friendliness and neighborliness from a dozen locations. Some of these neighboring houses are better than mine, some not quite so good. None of us would willingly move away."

My family didn't move to an official state residence because Vermont doesn't have one. Our telephone number remained in the book. I did get the occasional call at midnight from someone who'd had too much to drink and wanted me to settle a dispute with the neighbors, but people don't abuse that kind of thing much in Vermont. Recently, I got a call on a Sunday morning from a steelworker in Youngstown, Ohio, who asked what he could do to support me in my run for president.

As governor, I led a relatively normal life. I went to the supermarket and pumped my own gas. I remained the active parent of two kids, often driving them to school in a carpool, although usually with a trooper. I was very involved in their schools and went to their hockey and soccer games. There was never a large entourage around me, usually only one trooper for security standing inconspicuously in the distance.

I did sneak out sometimes without telling the troopers. Once, I went sailing in my Sunfish and got becalmed on the lake, and nobody knew where I was. I had to paddle back to shore. It wasn't fair to the people whose job it was to look after me, so I never did that again. But I did feel the need to be a real human being. Even Richard Nixon was said to sneak out of the White House and get pizza in the middle of the night once in a while.

In 1991, Vermont had the largest deficit in its history and also the highest marginal income tax in the United States. In the previous two years, taxes had been raised by $150 million, or 24 percent of the entire General Fund budget, as part of a deficit reduction package. I cut the taxes.

I'm not a big tax cutter. I think President Bush has harmed the country and raised middle-class property taxes with his tax cuts, but having the highest marginal income tax in America was having a terrible effect on Vermont's economy.

I knew the long-term answer to the recession was job creation. We had to cut taxes because businesses would not invest in the state. We couldn't attract the workers they needed because it was costing people so much to live. So we cut taxes by 30 percent over the lifetime of my administration. However, we didn't engage in the outrageous tax cutting that went on in some of the states. My feeling was, if you run a state properly, you attract investments. We did, and ended up creating tens of thousands of jobs in the ten years after 1991.

Governor Snelling had instituted a deficit reduction package that included a large tax increase, a measure he felt was necessary to balance the budget. He had to get the package through a Democratic house, and the tax hikes were the price he had to pay for the cuts he was going to impose at the same time. The agreement was that the taxes would automatically expire in two years.

But the economic situation was even worse than Governor Snelling thought. I began to cut spending programs, and the liberal Democrats in the house objected. They wanted to make the higher tax rate permanent. I said no, absolutely not under any circumstances. I told them I would veto it; we couldn't compete with tax rates so high.

The package of tax reductions and the balancing of the state budget got me off to a great start. There had been an expectation among Democrats that I'd simply keep the tax rates as high as they were, and that I'd keep spending. When I did neither, the liberals in the party were furious. In the end, though, all the Democrats were on board. In the current recession, we haven't had to cut higher education, K–12 education, or health care.

During my all my years in office, I was one of the toughest governors in the country on spending issues. Vermont is the only state that doesn't require a balanced budget in its constitution, but I balanced every budget when I was governor—eleven in all.

My tax cuts were absolutely different from President

Bush's. We had very high taxes compared with other states, and the tax cuts were part of a budget-balancing program that restored the fiscal health of the state. This president has deliberately driven the budget out of balance, using tax cuts in order to starve programs like Social Security, Medicare, and Medicaid. Far from building deficits the way President Bush has done, we eliminated the state deficit. Long-term deficits of the kind this president has put into place can undo an entire country. We have already lost three million private sector jobs since President Bush has been in office.

I've run in eight statewide races in Vermont, and I've won all of them. Vermont is one of only two states that elect governors for two-year terms (New Hampshire is the other). This ensures that governors are especially account-able, since they're up for reelection so regularly. I received plenty of Democratic support and plenty of independent support, but I also used to get between 30 and 40 percent of the Republican vote. Like everywhere else, the G.O.P. in Vermont is generally controlled by the right wing, but most Republican voters in the state are reasonable people. Republicans supported me primarily for the kind of fis-cally responsible measures I instituted when I first got into office.

I also received a lot of support in the business commu-nity and from moderates who knew they could trust me with their money and who weren't upset by my socially pro-gressive initiatives, since they never threatened to get out of hand and wreck the finances of the state. In time, I could give an inaugural address and talk about the expansions that manufacturing companies like Nastec, Mack Molding, ETSI, IDX, and Husky carried out in Vermont.

I decided to keep Governor Snelling's people in place. I thought it would have been wrong to fire my predecessor's appointees. The voters had elected him, not me. For example, Susan Auld was Snelling's commissioner of Labor and Industry. This was the same woman I'd defeated in a very difficult race for lieutenant governor in 1986. When I took over, I kept Susan on and she stayed for seven years.

Another valuable member of the Snelling cabinet was Con Hogan. He had been a turnaround specialist from the private sector, and he was probably the best Agency of Human Services secretary up until that time. He put in benchmarks so that we could measure the efficacy of the human services programs. If you invest dollars in such-and-such a program, for example, does teen pregnancy go down? Nobody had ever done that in human services before, and we desperately needed the information.

As soon as I became governor, in addition to fixing the budget and making the necessary tax cuts, I took the first opportunity that presented itself to try to do something about health care. I've always believed every American should have health care, even when I was in medical school. We are far behind every other industrialized country; it is pathetic that we're in this position.

When I first took office, Governor Roy Romer of Colorado, who was one of my mentors, appointed me as head of a National Governors Association task force on health care. This was an important job: Health care was a thorny issue then, as it is now. We went to see the bipartisan leadership in Congress. Tom Foley, who was Speaker of the House, was there. Bob Michel, the House minority leader, was there. He was a wonderful person. Newt Gingrich was there. He's not a wonderful person. Henry Waxman, a very, very bright man who has dedicated his career to health care for all, was there.

The time came for me to speak. I told them there were federal laws that were preventing states from implementing universal health care, and I asked them to get rid of the obstacles. They replied that there were a lot of people around Washington who'd built their careers on the notion that they were going to do something about health care. I said, "Well, in that case, can't you pass legislation to get universal health insurance?"

They said, "We can't pass anything," and I said, "Well, in that case, can you let *us* pass something?"

And the answer was "No, we can't."

Now, Tom Foley had been in the House of Representatives since 1965 and had been the whip and the majority leader and was the Speaker of the House while I was a freshman governor. Nevertheless, I told him hotly, "I think I'd have a different approach to health care if I was the head of an organization that had a twenty-seven percent favorability rating."

"No," he said, laughing, "it's really twenty-eight percent."

Tom Foley is a tremendous person whom I like very much, and I really had no business speaking to him in that way. It is not an incident I'm proud of now, but I was so impassioned that I felt compelled to speak at the time.

I was acting like a doctor. I have always been very results-oriented and not particularly process-oriented. I have found that it helps to cut to the chase in government, especially since one of the problems with government is that there tends to be too much process and too little result. Washington is paralyzed, and when it's not paralyzed, it's dismantling the things that are important to people.

I learned a valuable lesson that day in Washington. I realized I couldn't cut the Gordian knot of national health care by appealing to Congress. But it didn't stop me from trying in Vermont, and when our efforts at instituting universal health care fell short, we later went back and secured coverage for children.

CHAPTER

★ **9** ★

The entire time I was governor, I was never really able to catch my breath. After my first term in the house I had run unopposed, which I assumed was because I was in the community so much. I figured that what had worked for me as a legislator would work as governor, so I traveled the state relentlessly. We used to "shoot the circuit," as I called it, all the time, especially if we were campaigning. The trip was Burlington to White River to Brattleboro to Bennington to Rutland and back to Burlington, which is about four hundred miles. We would put 80,000 miles on a Mercury Marquis and 40,000 on a Ford Explorer in a year.

It could be tough for my staff whenever I was driving around the state. I'd look out the window, notice a problem, and call the responsible cabinet secretary. I'd make a list of everything I saw and call up later to see if the broken sign I'd seen three months previously had been fixed yet.

Much to the consternation of the long-suffering state troopers who traveled with me, I decided that driving to Boston for business made more sense than flying. Later, to their even greater dismay, I started driving to New York, as well. The car ride was a great opportunity to get some work done, especially once mobile phones came along, and there was no danger of getting trapped in an impromptu meeting. I got a lot of reading done.

When I went to schools, kids would ask me what being governor was like. I'd tell them it's like school: We have a foot-thick stack of homework every night, with files to read and papers to sign. The kids' faces always fell.

When it came time to look at health care in the state, I had years of practical experience of working within the system.

When I was doing my residency in Burlington, I had volunteered for a clinic in the North End of town. The clinic became the community health center and provided care to people with no health insurance. This was in the early eighties, a period of significant economic upheaval, and I saw quite a number of Vermonters who had recently lost their jobs and their health benefits. They were drawing on whatever savings they might have to get by day-to-day, and they certainly didn't have enough money to see a physician. I saw that a child with strep might be given Tylenol rather than be taken to the doctor for a proper diagnosis and treatment. Of course, if you can make regular trips to the doctor, not only do you avoid undertreating or ignoring potentially serious issues but you can also benefit from a range of wellness programs. I saw again that there were far too many families who lacked basic health care coverage.

Before I became governor, Vermont had a plan that covered children under six who weren't eligible for Medicaid. In 1992, we extended the children's program to age eighteen and to families earning the equivalent of $55,200 for a family of four. In 1995, we launched the Vermont Health Access Plan, which combined federal and state dollars to offer basic health insurance to working people with incomes up to $27,600 a year for a family of four. In 1998, families at 300 percent of the poverty level were included.

The children's program is called "Dr. Dynasaur," and it's an achievement I am very proud of. In our efforts to extend health care coverage, we did also go back and secure more prescription benefits. Low-income elderly and disabled people can get limited coverage up to 225 percent of the federal poverty level. They also have access to all the medicine they need at a discount of 41 percent off the retail price.

I recall one striking example of what programs like Dr. Dynasaur can achieve. A school in Bennington set up a dentist's office that treated fifty-seven eligible kids its first month. Six children who'd never been to a dentist before had to go to the emergency room and have decayed teeth extracted. One sixth-grader later told his principal he never knew what it felt like not to be in pain.

While the number of uninsured Americans has been

climbing, over the last ten years the rate of people who have no health insurance in Vermont has actually dropped from 17 percent to just under 8.5 percent. This means that almost 92 percent of our people now have coverage. Of everything we managed to achieve in health care in the state, I am proudest of this fact: 99 percent of all Vermont children are eligible for health insurance and 96 percent have it.

A key feature of childhood policy in Vermont has been our Success by Six program. When I was first governor, I was on the National Education Goals Panel. The first goal was that every child should arrive in school ready to learn. The rest of the objectives were concerned with high achievement in math or science and so forth, but we can't even begin to think about these when children are still going to school hungry.

Success by Six offers remedies. Vermont offers a home visit to every child in the state, no matter what the economic circumstances of the family. Ninety-one percent of families say "yes" and are visited. Local agencies choose who makes the visit, and I think it is especially beneficial when the school nurse comes to see the family. The nurse is able to establish a connection with the family at the time of the birth of a child who, three to five years later, will be in the school system.

When I became governor in 1991 and we were talking about spending, I asked state officials where they might be able to save money. The commissioner of corrections came to me and said he had to have a 14 percent budget increase. The price of our Success by Six program is $100 per child per year; the price of a jail cell is about $28,000 a year. What we have done in Vermont is, essentially, reduce the size of the cohort of kids who can't succeed in school by 43 percent. There has already been a significant downturn in placements for foster care for kids under twelve. Ten years from now, when those kids turn twenty, there ought to be a significant decline in the prison population.

While I was governor, I focused a great deal of attention on children and education. I believe that a state or society can be judged by the way it treats its children. If you are respectful of children and their opinions, they will be respectful of others when they grow up. I was very happy with the progress we made in education. Vermont has some of the smallest class sizes in the nation, for example—an average of 12.3 kids per class in 2000.

Special education was one of the most emotionally powerful programs I was associated with as governor. We began an effort to mainstream kids with disabilities. To begin with, we made sure that teachers would get enough help in the classroom from skilled paraprofessionals so that every child would benefit. The program has been a tremendous success. Vermont has 82 percent of all kids with Individualized Education Plans in mainstream schools. (IEPs are the main provision of the Individuals with Disabilities Education Act.) The national average is 48 percent.

Also noteworthy is a high school in Springfield, Vermont, that could serve as a model for others around the country. Representatives from the school came to Montpelier and said they would like some money to upgrade their school. Together, we transformed the school. We integrated the local community college into the vocational school. We set up programs so that vocational and high school kids could take college courses while they're in the high school and allow adults continuing their education to take courses with high schools kids. And with long-distance learning, we made sure that students can take courses from all over the country from their school in Springfield.

The school got a significant investment of funds from the state, much more than they would have received had they just upgraded their classrooms. Attached to the high school they built a vocational school that's governed by a community group of businesspeople and educators rather than the school board. And the community college moved into the high school. Now there is an educational establishment in Springfield, Vermont, where kids can go and take academic courses that lead them to college. They can also do apprenticeship courses, get college credits while they are in high school, and take courses from across the country while people from all over America can take courses that the school offers.

In January 2002, the new Howard Dean Education Center was dedicated. I am a little embarrassed but at the same time very pleased to say that the facility in Springfield is named after me. I am extremely proud to have my name on this wonderful example of cooperation among education, government, business, and the community.

In one of my State of the State addresses I talked about planning in government. I talked about two-year plans and five-year plans that are about the kinds of things that happen every month in the legislature. They are concerned with the budget or planning and yearly fights about how much money to spend on education. It is all in the short-term.

Then I mentioned twenty-year plans that are concerned with how to take care of kids. If you want to reduce the number of kids in jail and increase the number of kids in college, you have to start now for the generation we want to be in college, rather than in jail, in twenty years.

But for the environment, you need to have a one-hundred-year plan. Vermont has a strong tradition of protecting its environment and I worked to maintain that tradition. I am happy to say that we protected more than 470,000 acres of land—nearly 8 percent of the whole state—so that the land would always be available for public use. This land can still be timbered in a sustainable way. It can still be farmed on and would still be available for hunting and snowmobiling and hiking and camping. There are also wilderness areas that are set aside and will never be developed.

During my time as governor, Vermont made tremendous progress on a number of environmental issues, including energy efficiency, a subject of great interest to me. We created bike paths throughout the state and worked to ease pressure on the roads by bringing the first commuter rail train back to the state since the 1950s. We were the first state to subsidize Amtrak. We also worked hard to reduce pollution and increase energy conservation. Our Efficiency Vermont program has stopped one million tons of greenhouse gas emissions and generated $66.8 million in energy savings. The program meets 2 percent of the state's electricity needs. Businesses have seen an average return of 65 percent on their energy-efficient investments. I also ordered that emissions in the state be reduced to levels below those mandated by the Kyoto Protocol.

I closed seventy-six local unlined landfills, and we now require double-lined landfills with collection sewers in the state. I also played a lead role with the Conference of New England Governors and Eastern Canadian Premiers to address the threat of mercury pollution in the water in the region.

I was very concerned as governor that we make our urban areas livable. (The bike path in Burlington was what got me involved in politics in the first place.) Sprawl is one of the blights on our landscape. We worked to ensure that planning was intelligently integrated under the auspices of a development cabinet that included the heads of the transportation, natural resources, commerce, and agriculture agencies. A Downtown Bill I signed gave money to towns that centered development in existing urban areas. We advocated new federal buildings like courthouses and post offices in town centers to encourage development there and worked to limit unregulated sprawl in outlying areas.

We did these things because a hundred years from now the population of Vermont will probably be three times what it is now. If you want Vermont to continue to be Vermont, you have got to take a long-term vision. There's no long-term vision in the Bush administration in any area. I can't think of *any* serious long-term planning that they have done, certainly not when it comes to the environment.

• • •

People do pay attention to governors, even in Congress. The National Governors Association fought hard against the Democrats and even harder against the Republicans. If there's one thing governors of both parties hate, it is an unfunded mandate; congressmen of both parties, on the other hand, love them. This president is famous for them. An unfunded mandate means that state and local governments use their tax revenue for programs that the federal government wants but is unwilling to fund.

The respective responses of the two parties to unfunded mandates perfectly illustrate the striking difference between them. When the Democrats controlled the National Governors Association (I was chair of the NGA from 1994 to 1995), we used to fight against our own party when it passed legislation that harmed the states. When the Republicans took over, however, they took orders from the G.O.P. in Washington, with few standing up for the people they represented.

There were exceptions. I thought John Engler of Michigan would be extremely loyal to the national party, but he stood up to the Bush White House. Most Republican governors caved to the right-wing Republican White House because they were fearful; the folks in the White House are more than willing to threaten them.

I worked on recruiting and campaign support for the Democratic Governors' Association for six years, so I know most of the Democrats well. I liked many of them: Roy Romer is one, Tom Vilsack of Iowa another. I recruited Jim

Hodges from South Carolina to run, and he did a great job even though he didn't get reelected. He was a good governor and a hard worker. I enjoyed working with Angus King from Maine, an Independent who was governor from 1995 to 2003.

Janet Napolitano from Arizona, a former state attorney general, is terrific—she's going to be really outstanding, a star. John Kitzhaber of Oregon, a physician, was another governor whose word you could rely upon. That's a quality I value a great deal, both in politics and in my personal life. I can have strong disagreements with somebody, but if he can look me in the eye, tell me the truth, and keep his word, that means a lot to me.

Thomas Chittenden, the first governor of Vermont, served seventeen one-year terms. By 2002, I'd been governor longer than anyone other than Chittenden and was the longest-serving Democratic governor in the country.

I was proud of what we had achieved. We had balanced the budget and Vermont was in fine fiscal shape, with no deficit and $100 million in the bank. The tax rate was no longer the highest in the nation. We had secured health care for virtually all children under eighteen, and our early-intervention program saw child abuse rates drop dramatically. Our land conservation program would preserve the rural character of the state I had come to love.

By the end of August 2001, I was sure that I didn't want to run for reelection again. I called the cabinet together and told them, and they gave me a standing ovation. I was overwhelmed. These were the men and women who had implemented everything and for whose ideas I sometimes got credit. It was difficult to say good-bye to them. I publicly announced my intention right away. As much as I loved being governor, I was ready for a new challenge.

CHAPTER

★ 10 ★

Nothing has brought Judy and me more joy than raising our children together. I was present at the deliveries of both Anne and Paul, and each was an unforgettable experience. My perspective on the world changed as soon as my daughter was born. Once I was a father, parenthood was the most important thing in the world to me.

I've remained as committed as I can be to the outdoors life. I hiked the entire 270-mile Long Trail, which runs the length of the state, from the Canadian border to Massachusetts. Anne and Paul came about half the way. Paul and I also sailed the 110-mile length of Lake Champlain in the Sunfish.

We used to go camping regularly. There would be eight adults and about fourteen kids, ages five to nineteen, spread among ten canoes. My brother Bill would bring some or all of his five kids. We would paddle down the Connecticut River in a big flotilla and stop and pitch tents for the night. Paul, Anne, and I have canoed the river's entire length, about four hundred miles, over a series of weekends and holidays spanning five years.

It's a wonderful trip. We started at Indian Stream in the north and traveled down the river past Pittsburg, New Hampshire. The river marks the boundary between Vermont and New Hampshire and finally emerges into Long Island Sound. As soon as we canoed through the upper Connecticut River, I knew I wanted to help save it. Both states are now signing easements to protect thirty-three miles of shoreline. It will never be developed.

Paul and Anne have grown up leading a reasonably normal life, even though I've been governor for such a long time. In fact, they can hardly remember when I wasn't governor. We have always done a lot of things together, and security worked hard not to be too intrusive.

I used to coach hockey when I first became governor. I coached the smallest teams, the so-called house teams, which are for the youngest kids in organized hockey. My daughter and my son were on the team, which was pretty good. Despite my enthusiasm, I really didn't know that much about the game. I was good at keeping order, and I had played enough to know a little more than the rudiments. But I knew if the team wanted to progress, they'd need a different coach.

This suspicion was confirmed one day when I was making line changes in the middle of a game. My son and my daughter are both nice, mild-mannered kids. On this occasion, however, they saw what I was doing, and they jumped up and shouted in unison as loud as they could, "Dad! Dad! You don't know what you're doing!" I knew then that my coaching career was very near its end, and indeed it did come to its inglorious conclusion shortly thereafter. Paul still plays and is the captain of his high school team, as Anne was before him.

It is important to me in this campaign to protect the privacy of my family. I have had real disagreements with journalists about the role that families play in campaigns. I think the national press has behaved better over the last two presidencies with respect to the First Family. The national press acted reasonably toward Chelsea Clinton, and they are good with the Bush girls, with one exception. I know that several thousand kids every year get caught with false IDs. For the media to cover the children of the president with the same scrutiny as their parents is wrong.

My kids are very independent. We're a very close family, and they're in the middle of what eighteen-year-olds and seventeen-year-olds do around that age, which is figure out what kinds of adults they will become. They don't need hundreds of people inspecting them as they do that. I'm going to be very protective of their privacy both now and during any Dean administration.

My wife is an independent woman, as well. She is a doctor, and a very, very good one. Her patients think she is terrific. At the same time, Judy is very supportive of me and my campaign. She's made videos, she's done interviews, and she'll do more as long as it doesn't interfere with her medical practice. If we win, she'll move her medical practice to Washington.

I support Judy just as strongly as she supports me. There has been some criticism of Judy's decision not to give up her medical practice, but there has also been a good deal of praise. Many couples in America now have both partners working. The 2000 census reported there were 56.5 million married couples in the United States, and both partners worked in more than 30 million of those marriages. The notion that the wife is going to be dragged along in the wake of her husband's career is something that should have been left behind decades ago.

My wife has a great career, and she is very good at what she does. She's going to be a great doctor whether I make it to the White House or not. There are going to be a lot of people in America, particularly women, who applaud her. But there will be some who don't. I hope they respect her decision.

I'm a fairly religious person though I don't regularly attend church or temple. I'm a Christian; my church is Congregationalist, a traditional New England denomination that is quite decentralized. Individual parishes call their own minister and more or less govern themselves.

I pray just about every day. I have a prayer for everyone who is in trouble. I also believe that good and evil exist in the world, and I thoroughly disapprove of people who use religion to inflict pain on others.

One of the shortest answers I will ever give follows the question of what I like to do to relax. Whenever I'm home, we'll have dinner together as a family, which is time that I relish. But I was never very good at relaxing.

When I'm at home, I work around the house. As far as television is concerned, I only watch the news. The books I read these days tend to be historical in nature, though I do have a weakness for physics—quantum physics, molecular physics, and astrophysics. I'm not a physicist at all; I don't do the higher math and I couldn't explain string theory, but I'm addicted to the "Science" section of *The New York Times*.

I'll often be asked which books have affected me. One of the greatest political books I've read is Robert Penn Warren's *All the King's Men*. The book is based on the life of Huey Long, the populist Louisiana governor and senator who was murdered in 1935. Long was originally chosen as a third-party candidate to siphon off votes from someone the bosses didn't want, and he turned out to be a larger-than-life figure who dominated politics in his state. The lesson I took from the book was: Be careful what you wish for; you may get it.

Harper Lee's *To Kill a Mockingbird* meant a lot to me. The book's theme is racial justice in the South, and Atticus Finch is the paradigm of a guy who is willing to stand up for what is right. *Sometimes a Great Notion* by Ken Kesey is an extraordinary voyage by a counterculture writer into an America of the past that wasn't countercultural at all.

There is a book I think every American should read. It's called *Nickel and Dimed*, and it was written by Barbara Ehrenreich. If you think the discussion about the travails of the middle class and the working poor is a liberal invention, you must read this book. It demonstrates exactly how hard it is to get by in America, and how much harder it is as a single mom. The author was a waitress, a chambermaid, and worked at a Wal-Mart; in the process, she found out how difficult it is to make ends meet when you have no benefits, no sick pay, and no chance to change your schedule if you need to. There are millions of Americans in the same situation. By and large, they don't vote because they've given up on the system. The Democrats haven't done enough for them, and the Republicans don't care.

Harry S. Truman is my great political hero, and David McCullough's biography is a truly magnificent book. I read *Truman* to Anne and Paul when they were in the second and third grades, and they both loved it. It is one of the books that has had the most impact on me in the last ten years.

Harry Truman was an authentic American hero. He was a real person who had the ability to connect with people because he lived the life of an ordinary American. Truman had to follow FDR, the most important figure in twentieth-century American history, and he acquitted himself extraordinarily well. Truman acted with clarity and firmness, and he was willing to make unpopular decisions if he knew they'd be good for the long-term future of the country.

Truman recalled General Douglas MacArthur, an extremely unpopular decision at the time, but one that reasserted the principle of civilian control over the military. Another decision that I greatly admire was the integration of the armed forces, which was disliked with equal intensity in the North and the South. Truman was born in Missouri in 1884, only twenty years after Missouri had been a slave-owning state, yet Truman confronted racism when FDR had sometimes tiptoed around it. In 1948, Truman stood up for a principle that was not addressed until more than twenty years later and is still not fully resolved today, the idea that all Americans should be truly equal under the law. I'm certain that Truman influenced my thinking on the civil unions bill.

Of the great presidents, I would rank Washington first, followed by Lincoln and FDR. The next four, in no particular order, would be Jefferson, Truman, Theodore Roosevelt, and Lyndon Johnson. I disliked LBJ intensely because of the Vietnam War, but looking back, he was one of the most important presidents in American history due to his involvement in civil rights, the War on Poverty, and the creation of Medicare. He remade America and gave hope to those who had no voice.

I do enjoy working around the house, taking care of necessary chores like mowing the lawn and taking out the trash.

I hate spending money on fixing up the house; I would much rather try to do it myself, although the results are not always exactly what I hoped for. Stories abound about how cheap I am; they're all true. The good news is, I was cheap with the taxpayers' money before, and I will be again.

I don't indulge myself when it comes to clothes, either. I have a suit that cost $125 at JCPenney in 1987. My suits are like my friends: They're with me for the long haul. When I travel I have a rule: no checked luggage. I went on a trip to Argentina recently, and the one suit I took was my '87 JCPenney. My great traveling companion was A. Wayne Roberts, who worked in the Reagan White House and is now head of the Lake Champlain Regional Chamber of Commerce. I wore the suit every day for two weeks. I'm not in the same place for more than two days. Who's going to notice? Every day Wayne would say, "There's that suit again."

Wayne was determined to get me to throw the suit out, and he nearly succeeded. "Why don't you burn it?" he said. "We'll have a ceremony." I actually agreed and threw the suit into the closet the night before its planned demise. The next day, I pulled out the suit and it had a perfect crease. I was delighted. I told Wayne I couldn't burn a suit that holds a perfect crease.

I came home, and the suit was a disaster. "Perhaps its time really has come," I thought. I decided not to have it dry-cleaned—why bother?—so I threw it in the washing machine to see what would happen. The suit came out with no wrinkles whatsoever. Who's going to throw away a suit like that? I still have it to this day.

• • •

Once a year, the nation's governors are invited to a black-tie White House dinner. I was always proud to represent Vermont at events like this, but I've always hated wearing a tuxedo. In fact, I've used the same one I've had since high school. It still fits, more or less, and I'm not about to waste a thousand dollars on a new one.

I'm about twenty pounds heavier than I was in high school—I used to wrestle at 147 pounds—so I'd have to shoehorn myself into this tuxedo every year. I'd walk around with my chest stuck out and my waist held in. I must have been blue in the face.

One year I had a bad cough. I got through the dinner, but soon afterward, I felt a tickle in my throat. As I coughed, my pants ripped open in the front. The only thing holding me together was the cummerbund. I buttoned my coat, tightened everything up, and held my hands in front. I called the Vermont trooper and asked him to walk in front of me as we left the White House. I took the pants to the cleaners the next day and had the pants fixed for $25.

We live in a wonderful part of the world. We moved out of the North End of Burlington and found a lovely place to live near Lake Champlain. It's close to everything—the hospital where Judy and I studied, the school, the office, and the library. The lake is a block away, and our nine-mile bike path is even closer.

In many ways, we are a typical American family. Our

house is composed of four individuals who exhibit various stages of neatness—nonneatness, mostly. We all keep busy, so housekeeping is not a priority. On some days, it looks like a bomb went off in the house and there are clothes lying everywhere. When I get home from a trip, I just load the laundry into the hamper and reload my small carry-on from the last clean wash. We drive a Ford Explorer, which hopefully by the third year of my administration will be getting thirty-seven miles to the gallon. We're really a soccer-mom-and-dad—or more accurately, a hockey-mom-and-dad—family.

Vermont is a great place to bring up children. It has a good school system, the sixth best in the nation according to the National Assessment for Educational Progress. In Burlington, the schools are quite diverse, and signs in high schools are in English, Vietnamese, and Serbo-Croatian. Vermont is an extraordinarily egalitarian state. Nobody is better than anybody else, and it's a terrific place to enjoy an outdoor life.

CHAPTER

★ 11 ★

My life has been profoundly changed by the death of two people who were very close to me. The first was my brother Charlie in 1975, and the second was my father in 2001. These events had a tremendous effect on me, and they constitute a significant part of who I am.

There was some blessing in each case, because I don't have strong regrets about anything being left unsaid. But my brother's death did teach me that you should never go away without telling somebody you love them, because you never know if you're going to see them again.

My brother and I were close when we were growing up. We were only sixteen months apart, and consequently, we fought a lot. We played sports together, along with the other kids, but there was a good deal of rivalry between us. Charlie was a natural leader with tremendous charisma; he was elected president of the school we all went to. He was very bright, but he had too much fun politicking to do too much academically.

Many things about Charlie impressed me. I remember him giving his last speech as school president at his graduation dinner. Just before he was due to speak, I saw Charlie sitting at the head table writing away. He was a terrible procrastinator, so I assumed he just wasn't prepared. He then stood up and gave an extraordinarily polished speech. I was astonished that an eighteen-year-old kid could do that. To this day, I tend to write my speeches five minutes before I give them, if I write them at all, but they aren't as well organized as his was that evening.

Even at prep school, Charlie exhibited an uncommon maturity. As school president, he had significant influence in disciplinary matters. The faculty had veto power, but he and the headmaster made a lot of decisions about whether someone was going to stay in school or be suspended or expelled. He handled that responsibility extremely well.

He went to the University of North Carolina at Chapel Hill as a political science major. I've been to Chapel Hill many times and taken both my kids to look at it—it's a great school. As Charlie and I got older, we became very close. I went down to stay with him, and he called me when there were problems in his life he thought I could be helpful with. He hadn't done that before I was at college. I was grateful for the time Charlie and I had after high school. The childhood rivalry was gone, and we became genuine friends as well as brothers.

Charlie did well at UNC and was involved in the student government. I always believed that he would have gone to law school and ended up in politics. After college, Charlie set off on a trip abroad. When you leave college, you're unencumbered and you have a chance to see something of the world. Once you have a job and a wife and children, it's much harder to find the time. I have always had some guilt because I advised Charlie to travel.

On the first leg of his trip, Charlie sailed to Japan as a passenger on a freighter. He stayed for a few weeks and then took another freighter to Australia. He lived for nine months with a friend on a ranch by the Pascoe River, north of Cairns on the northern tip of Queensland, clearing land. He then went to Indonesia and on to the Southeast Asian country of Laos to visit a friend of our father's who worked for USAID. Together with an Australian named Neal Sharman, Charlie stayed in a little bungalow on the Mekong River. He planned to meet up with a friend who was with the Peace Corps in Nepal eventually.

Laos in 1974 was incredibly dangerous; in neighboring Vietnam, Saigon had not yet fallen and the war was raging. U.S. forces bombed the daylights out of Laos because the Ho Chi Minh Trail, which was the supply line from North Vietnam to South Vietnam, went directly through the country. Additionally, Laos was in the middle of its own three-way war between pro-Western, neutralist, and pro-Communist factions. The Communist Pathet Lao guerrillas had been fighting with the Viet Minh in the area since the 1950s; they eventually prevailed and took power in 1975.

This was the situation while Charlie was visiting. He

wrote me a letter about what it was like to sit outside his bungalow at night, listening to the thump of distant artillery and the muffled explosions as the shells hit the ground. I almost wrote him back, saying, "What are you thinking? Get out of there—it's not safe." Then I reminded myself that he was a twenty-three-year-old who was capable of making these judgments himself. I've often wished I had written that letter, although I don't think he would have changed his mind had he read it.

There was speculation that Charlie was in Laos because he was working for the CIA and I think my parents believed that to be the case. Personally, I don't think he was employed by the U.S. government in any capacity, but we'll probably never know the answer to that question.

By October 1974, I had moved back in with my parents and was studying for medical school. Charlie had been away from the country for some time; we hadn't heard from him in three months, and we were very worried. We'd been writing his friend in Nepal to see if Charlie had shown up. He hadn't.

One day, around ten o'clock in the morning, the phone rang in the apartment. The voice on the other end of the line said, "Is this Mr. Howard Dean?"

I said, "Yes."

It was someone from the State Department. He said, "We have information that shows that Mr. Charles Dean, your son, is a captive of the Pathet Lao." I told him he'd better call my father, which he did. For my parents' sake, I'm glad I was home during the following seven months, but they were some of the most awful months of my life.

We were all shocked that Charlie had been captured, and we began trying everything we could to secure his release. The CIA and the U.S. military provided us with tremendous amounts of information about Charlie, and for that reason, I will always have immense respect for them.

Charlie was classified as a POW-MIA, although we don't know why. It's a good thing he was, because it allowed the U.S. military to do all that they have done for our family over the last twenty-five years. In that time, I've had a window into what it is like to be a family member of somebody who disappeared, died, or was wounded.

In the beginning, we were getting streams of information coming out of Pathet Lao–held territory from people who could freely cross between the zones. We knew where Charlie was, we knew what kind of condition he was in, and we knew what his daily routine was like. We found out that Charlie had indeed been taken by the Pathet Lao. Charlie and Neal had decided to take a raft down the Mekong River to Thailand. On September 5, 1974, they were stopped at a checkpoint near a small village called Pak Him Boun, just two miles southeast of the capital of Laos, Vientiane. The Pathet Lao took the two of them away, apparently because they were carrying cameras. Charlie managed to have a picture of himself smuggled out to the embassy in Vientiane, which alerted us to his plight.

In December 1974, my father went to Laos and tried to

meet with Communist officials to persuade them to set Charlie free. He was worried about the meager diet that prisoners were fed and about the risks of diseases like dysentery and malaria. My father left a package of medicine and clothing for Charlie and Neal with Pathet Lao officials, but we've never known if it reached them. In the meantime, we discovered later, Charlie was insisting he be taken to the caves at Sam Neua, in the northern part of the country, where the Pathet Lao had its headquarters. We assume he figured he wasn't able to get anyone locally to make a decision about letting him go.

In February 1975, my mother went to Laos. My father hadn't made much progress on his trip in December, so she was hoping for any news at all. By that time, we had no idea what had happened to Charlie. My mother met one of the Pathet Lao ministers. She said he had looked sideways at her; he wouldn't look her in the eye. She concluded then that Charlie had already been killed. We received notification in May that she was probably right.

Later, we were able to piece together details of what must have happened. Around December 14, 1974, Charlie and Neal were put in a truck and driven away. Witnesses saw the two young men being loaded onto the truck. The next day, the vehicle came back empty, with only the handcuffs that Neal and Charlie had been held with lying in the truck. We assume that Charlie and Neal were executed on or about December 14, 1974.

When I first found out Charlie was probably dead, I was about to take an organic chemistry test. I couldn't think of anything else I could do, so I left the apartment, got on the bus, and went to Columbia to take the exam. I was in a complete daze, and got a 50 on the test. It was a dreadful test that everybody flunked—and for different reasons than I did—and the whole class had to retake it.

Charlie's capture and death were the most traumatic events of my life. They have eaten at me ever since. You never get over something like this; all you can do is live with it. It was awful for my two other brothers and me, and it was far worse for our mother and father. It was so painful for my father that he rarely spoke of it afterward. My brothers and I worked for a long time with the Department of Defense and the State Department, looking for information; we shared little of that with my father. He deserved the chance to deal with this in his own way. My mother was more like her sons. She had a way of coping that my father never found.

My father died in August 2001 at the age of eighty, over a quarter century after his son had been taken. He had chronic medical problems, largely as a result of diabetes that hadn't been very well-controlled for quite some time; he ended up with kidney and congestive heart failure. Dad got very sick on Memorial Day. He was taken to the local hospital in Southampton, but he was too ill to be treated there, so they transferred him to Stony Brook Hospital, the nearest major medical center.

My chief of staff, Julie Peterson, had a great insight. Her father had dropped dead of a heart attack at the age of fifty-seven. She said if you take your time to die, it's easier on the family and much harder for you. If you die suddenly, it's easier on you, but much harder on the family. I think that is true. Of course, almost no one has a choice in the matter, but I doubt very much that my father would have chosen to go as he did; he was by no means ready to go.

In his last three months, I'd come down to see him and my mother every week; my brothers also came as often as they could. There was always somebody with my mother, but we all had jobs and families elsewhere. My brother Jim lived just across the Long Island Sound, and he was there the most. In retrospect, I think that the time we all had together was a godsend.

It was very hard to watch my father drift away, but it did give me time to get my thoughts in order. As a doctor, I knew what was happening to him. My family hoped against hope that he might pull through. I was in the position of explaining to them that the story was not likely to end well.

Eventually, his heart just gave out. We got him home for about two weeks, but he was so sick. He had to have round-the-clock nurses, and it was really a struggle. We had to take him back to the local hospital in Southampton, where he died about four days later.

In those three months, I had time to think about our relationship. I closed some loops that hadn't been addressed over the years. It might seem like an odd word to use, but this was a wonderful process for me. Our relationship had always been a complex and difficult one. I was the oldest son of an incredibly charismatic and magnetic person. He was not only the star of the family but a star in the community he grew up in. I was finally able to give something back to this remarkable, powerful person. That three-month period was a very important one in my life.

My friend David Berg told me once that how you die is important because you're teaching your kids how to die. There are ways you do it, and ways you shouldn't do it. I thought about that often as my father was dying.

Over the years, the family had kept in touch with the State Department, the CIA, and the Department of Defense about Charlie. We pushed for any scrap of information. Finally, in 2000, there was a break. Through accounts given by people who had seen the two young men killed, the site where Charlie and Neal were believed to have been buried was located.

In February 2002, I decided I would take some time for myself and fly to Vientiane. I wanted to see where Charlie had most likely died.

The countryside there is like no other I have ever seen. The most brilliantly green mountains stick straight up out of the plain. When I came back, I spoke to a group of veterans in Vermont about the place. They became emotional as we talked, and they recalled their service in Vietnam.

I took a helicopter ride down the Mekong River and over the plains and into the mountains along the Laotian border with Vietnam. The Ho Chi Minh Trail was visible, along with evidence of the heavy bombing during the war.

Even today, many of the people of Laos lead a primitive lifestyle, by American standards. The Lao are a very gentle people who have been victimized for generations by a series of bad governments. Laos is presently governed by a Communist dictatorship, but the government was courteous and hospitable to me, and they have been helpful in my brother's case.

When I got to Vientiane, something that had been troubling me for years was resolved. One of the feelings that accompanies survivor's guilt is anger at the person who was killed. You are angry because your loved one left you with this terrible loss. I had never understood why Charlie had gone to Laos and stayed there so long. As I said, I never believed he was working for the U.S. government. When I got to Vientiane, I immediately understood why he'd stayed. When I met the people and felt the pace of the city and learned how gentle and beguiling Southeast Asia was, I appreciated how he had been captivated by it.

I spent time in Laos with members of the Joint Task Force–Full Accounting. The JTF-FA was established in 1992. Young men and women from all four U.S. military branches volunteer to go and live for several weeks in the jungle and look for remains of Americans lost in the war in Southeast Asia.

There was an excavation site set up at the base of a mountain. A plane had been shot down and gone into the side of the hill. It was sobering to think of the enormous power of an airplane going into the side of a mountain or into a streambed at three hundred miles an hour. The Joint Task Force hires entire villages to sift through wreckage, put it in buckets, and bring it to a screening area, where the wreckage is searched for human remains.

I went to five of these sites. We stayed in a base camp at night and traveled out during the day to one of the sites. I was part of the bucket brigade, which brought earth to a central sifting site, and was also part of the screening team.

Life in the camp was great. The task force was just like America, with people of every race and religion. They were wonderful, caring people who had a mission and, furthermore, were very proud of that mission.

We found mostly pieces of equipment—shards of shattered metal and scraps of uniforms and webbing—but once in a while, someone would find a tooth or a piece of bone, and a huge cheer would erupt. Any samples would be taken to the U.S. Army Central Identification Laboratory in Hawaii (CILHI), which operates a DNA-matching lab. Families of POW-MIAs have been asked to provide DNA in case remains are found. My family has had our DNA at the lab for quite some time.

On my last day in Laos, we went to my brother's site. I knew roughly where it was; I had been looking at maps of the area for more than twenty-five years. As we traveled up the road, I saw the villages whose names were so familiar to me.

We were able to meet the farmer on whose land this took place, and we met the witness who had seen my brother's body and the body of his friend lying in the bomb crater where they were buried. In 1974, there had been a construction camp on the site for a North Vietnamese regiment that was building a road. We don't know exactly where Charlie is buried, and in the twenty-five-plus years since he died, what was a construction site has become a rice paddy.

The witness couldn't point out the precise location, but he knew there was a large rock nearby, which we found. The crater was supposed to be somewhere in the vicinity, but it had been bulldozed and plowed over.

We got more information from our witnesses. I think they were afraid to speak openly in front of the government representatives who were with us. Still, we were able to get one of the witnesses aside and away from his government minder. There was a U.S. Army interpreter who was a Thai-American and could speak the Lao dialect, so we were able to ask questions out of earshot of the Laotian government.

Some people had claimed that Charlie had been shot while trying to escape. That may be true. Others said he grew sick and died. But I don't believe that two young, healthy twenty-three-year-olds got sick and died on exactly the same day, even if they had been in captivity for three months.

I talked to the eyewitness, whom I'll call Mr. S. Unfortunately, since I'm not a lawyer, I made the mistake of leading the witness. We didn't have much time when we talked with him, so I asked Mr. S. whether the person who killed my brother was North Vietnamese. The place where Charlie had been killed was only about seven miles from North Vietnam, and in order to get to Sam Neua from the southern part of Laos, you'd have to go through North Vietnam. Mr. S. quickly said yes, it was a North Vietnamese. Of course, the witness was only too pleased to oblige me when I served up that option for him. Still, we don't know whether Charlie was killed by the North Vietnamese or someone else. For all I know, it could have been Mr. S. who shot him. He would have been a young soldier at the time. I gave gifts to the farmer and to the witnesses. I know that people involved in the POW-MIA effort from the other side are very worried about being punished for what they said or didn't say, or what they saw or didn't see. I wanted to make clear that our family was very grateful for the information.

A few years ago, what appeared to be a shin bone was recovered from the location where my brother is buried, but the DNA was insufficient to get a match. We don't know if it was part of my brother's body, his friend Neal's body, or even an animal.

This was one of the most emotional days of my life. As we were about to get in the helicopter to leave, I realized that I'd left something behind. I wanted to go back. I just stood there in front of where the bomb crater might have been, quietly for some time. These were very powerful moments, and for me, it did bring a feeling of closure.

Although I have spoken to counselors about my brother's death, in ways I still don't fully understand, it is a central episode in my life. It also isolates me to some extent, since there are only four people alive who went through it. Of course, relatives and friends grieved with us, but it has remained an unspoken bond among my mother and my two brothers and me. My brother and I have talked to our kids about it, but in some ways, it can't mean anything to them. They never knew Charlie.

I believe this experience sets me apart from many civilians in two ways. First, when I came out against the war in Iraq, I remained very supportive of the troops. I knew what it was like to have somebody close to me disappear and to worry desperately about what had happened. Second, it gave me great respect for the reality of war, though only people who have been in combat can truly understand it. I think the most extraordinary responsibility the president of the United States has is sending American kids to foreign countries to fight and perhaps to die.

I'd like to go back to Laos one more time. I'd like to take my mother and my brothers there. We're still hoping to recover remains, if there are any to be found. The place where Charlie is buried is an incredibly peaceful spot in the mountains, near a tiny creek that was diverted to irrigate a rice paddy.

I often think about the courses our lives might have taken had Charlie been around. One thing is certain: I'm sure that, had he lived, he'd be the one running for president and not me.

PART TWO

CHAPTER

★ 12 ★

I considered running for president in the 2000 election. I knew perfectly well that I would lose, but I wanted to affect the debate. I felt then, as I feel now, that no one was really talking about the issues dearest to me: health care and children. I decided against it that year primarily because, at that time, I believed my children were not old enough to handle the inevitable pressures they would be subjected to if I ran for national office. There was also more to be done in Vermont, in particular to secure the financial health of the state.

This time, however, I was driven by the policies of the current administration. I have been so dismayed by this president and the road he's taking the country down. I knew George W. Bush when we were both governors. I had always liked him, and he's smarter than people give him credit for. As governor, George W. Bush was always straightforward, something I appreciate in a person. And, by Texas standards, he was actually a moderate. He tried, for example, to reform the archaic tax system in his state, an effort that failed in the end but was well intended.

Since becoming president, however, George W. Bush has moved far to the right. He's pursued a truly radical agenda. He's led us into an unnecessary and costly war and is taking the country off an economic cliff with a reckless $3 trillion tax cut program. Meanwhile, he's cutting critical services for everyone from veterans to children, attacking our civil liberties, and dividing us along racial, economic, and gender lines. When I saw the full scope of this president's radical agenda, I knew I couldn't stand on the sidelines.

As governor, the two biggest motivations I had for getting up every morning were children and health care, the same two passions that compelled me to go to work every day as a doctor. I am also deeply worried about what is happening to the long-term financial future of our country. These were the issues I hoped to discuss as I went around the country: health care for every American, early childhood development, and a balanced budget that would bring financial stability and jobs back to America. While I knew it was a long shot, it was my hope that I would influence the debate enough to make a difference for families struggling to find health care and for children in those critical early years of their lives.

So, I began traveling the United States in 2002. I met people from all walks of life, from every background, in every possible circumstance. What I was hearing from these Americans began to change my thinking.

Everywhere I went, I was hearing a similar message from the people I was meeting. Sure, they wanted to talk about particular issues: health care, jobs, the war. But I was hearing a far deeper concern from Americans all across the country. Those I met were decent people, working hard to make ends meet and to build a better life for themselves and for their families. Again and again, they spoke of a larger fear about the future of the country.

Mostly they focused on the economy and a fear of losing their jobs, and of what that would mean for their children, their mortgages, their way of life. Unemployment reached 6.4 percent in the summer of 2003, the highest it's been in nine years. More than 3 million private-sector jobs have been lost since this president took office. More than 9.3 million Americans are looking for work and more than 2 million Americans have been looking for work for more than six months.

The problem is far deeper than just lost jobs. People are working harder for less money, and when they do lose their jobs, it's taking them longer to find other good ones. Many of them end up taking jobs that pay far less and now they're "underemployed." (Studies indicate that when a worker loses a manufacturing job, he takes a pay cut on average of 13 percent in his next job.) The statistics understate the depth of the economic crisis in the country.

And then there's the problem of health care. With health

care costs rising, more and more employers, especially small businesses, are finding it harder to insure their employees, leaving them vulnerable to an accident or an illness that can bankrupt an entire family. Millions of Americans are not getting the medical attention they need. Today, 41 million American men, women, and children lack health insurance. More than 40 percent of uninsured adults postponed seeking medical care in 2002 alone. The number of uninsured is soaring at the rate of nearly 1 million people every year.

The problems described by the Americans I've met run far deeper than the particular circumstance any one of them is facing. As Americans, as a country, we've built structures since the time of Franklin Delano Roosevelt to protect those of us who may be victimized by a layoff or a medical emergency or general economic hardship. Yet these structures are being systematically dismantled in this country by a political movement with a clear ideology and a relentless focus. The leaders of this movement are essentially saying to the American people, "Fend for yourselves."

The president's tax cuts are much more than simply a giveaway to friends and supporters. They are part of a master strategy to starve the core programs that have shaped our country's safety net for sixty years. And with this strategy, they are putting at risk the future of Social Security, Medicare, Medicaid, and countless other programs designed to ensure that our middle class stays strong and working families can make ends meet.

The long-term strategic goals of the tax-slashing "crusade" were described by Paul Krugman in an article called "The Tax-Cut Con" in *The New York Times Magazine*. Krugman identified two tax-cutting doctrines, both of which call for lower taxes for the very rich. Advocates of the strand of the argument that is called "supply-side" economics have claimed that tax cuts stimulate the economy and offset decreased government revenue so you don't have to cut programs to meet the deficit. But in reality, taxes are being cut specifically so that government programs have to be reduced and reduced drastically. The "supply-side" notion that services can be maintained is a platitude: The real object is to "starve the beast," in a phrase coined by David Stockman, Ronald Reagan's budget director.

In his article, Paul Krugman quotes Grover Norquist, president of Americans for Tax Reform who says, "I don't want to abolish government, I simply want to reduce it to the size where I can drag it into the bathroom and drown it in the bathtub."

This is starving the beast. And the way that the beast is reduced is by cutting off its lifeblood: tax revenue. What does this idea actually mean for Americans? For the wealthy few—a very few—it means significantly lower taxes. But for many, many more Americans, the consequence is actually *higher* taxes, as the burden of taxation is shifted from the few to the many.

However, the primary goal of this radical ideology goes far beyond tax cuts and shifting burdens. It is an assault on the institutions of government created by presidents like

Franklin Roosevelt and Lyndon Johnson, which have helped millions upon millions of Americans, programs like Social Security, Medicare, and Medicaid. Starving the government of money means these critical lifelines have to be reduced, eventually to the point where they can no longer help people, and those people who need the help will have nowhere to turn. The president's natural constituency, of course, is unlikely to ever look to the safety nets provided by Medicare, Medicaid, unemployment insurance, or Social Security—but they do get the overwhelming benefit of his tax cuts, which aim to exempt dividends, capital gains, and inheritance from any taxation. If this isn't radical, I don't know what is.

Paul Krugman says this ideology is now "firmly within the conservative mainstream." The president has expressed pleasure at the diminishing budget surplus. In August 2001, he said it was "incredibly positive news," because Congress would be left in a "fiscal straitjacket," one that might only be relieved in the long term by drastic cuts in programs.

It is worth quoting further from Paul Krugman's article. He paints a grim picture of the America that would exist if the tax-cutting zealots succeed and we revert to the minimalist government that prevailed before FDR:

> In [Grover] Norquist's vision, America a couple of decades from now will be a place in which elderly people make up a disproportionate share of the poor, as they did before Social Security. It will also be a country in which even middle-class elderly Americans are, in

many cases, unable to afford expensive medical procedures or prescription drugs and in which poor Americans generally go without even basic health care. And it may well be a place in which only those who can afford expensive private schools can give their children a decent education.

We do not have to look ahead a couple of decades to see the severe consequences of this administration's policies. Right now, millions of Americans are slipping down the economic ladder, and our middle class is shrinking. People everywhere are finding it harder not only to get ahead in this country but even to stay in the same place. Few in Washington recognize the problem or talk about it, but more and more Americans are growing alienated from our leadership, since no one in Washington seems to be discussing the issues that matter most to ordinary people.

That's why 50 percent of the people in this country have stopped voting. So many of them feel that they are talking and no one is listening, that politicians no longer care. So many Americans are afraid that something is fundamentally wrong in this country, but what really worries them is that they might not have the power to make it right.

This feeling of powerlessness is not unfounded. Our political leadership, particularly the current administration, has made a show of courting the wealthiest among us when deciding on the policies that affect all of us. It's no wonder ordinary Americans feel shut out of the political process. They've essentially been told that they cannot have access unless they pay for it.

Theirs is the very same fear that James Madison and Thomas Jefferson spoke about more than two hundred years ago: the fear that economic power would one day try to seize political power. At the very foundation of our country stands Democratic capitalism, a system which was always supposed to answer to the democracy and be subservient to it. In this type of democracy, the common good is more important than any individual or any one group. The rights of property were firmly established, and the principles of commerce and capitalism were rightly protected. Even special interests were recognized, but none of this was at the expense of democracy. As Theodore Roosevelt said, "Every special interest is entitled to justice—full, fair, and complete . . . but not one is entitled to a vote in Congress, to a voice on the bench or to representation in any public office."

In our system, power was placed in the hands of the people—"government of the people," as Abraham Lincoln described it. That is you and me, coming together at the polls to decide freely how our country is to be run. When government caters to the privileged few, democracy itself is undermined and the American people are no longer served. Our country now appears to be moving further toward the direction our founders feared: the prospect of government of the corporations, by the special interests, and for those who make the largest campaign contributions.

America was founded on the ethos that we are one community, and we are all in this together. Our current political leadership has broken down and degraded our sense of community, choosing instead to pursue policies that benefit only the individuals or corporations that fund their campaigns. This is not what democracy is supposed to look like.

What saddens me most is that I hear in the voices of the American people a pervasive sense of loss, a feeling that the America we grew up believing in no longer exists. Meeting and talking to thousands of people in living rooms, union halls, and diners across the country, I have heard anger and dismay about the direction in which our leaders have taken us. The country is in crisis.

I began traveling the country expecting to talk about issues that were dear to me, but I have come to see that what is happening in America is so much larger than any one issue to be raised in a policy debate. Americans feel set apart from one another and from their government, and there is a longing to reconnect.

We are now at a crossroads. The future will be about nothing less than the principles America was founded upon. Today we face three challenges. Our task is to bring people back into the political process and give them a democracy they can believe in once more, to rebuild the fractured American community, and to restore America's role as an idealistic moral force in the world.

CHAPTER

★ 13 ★

When the campaign started, I had no idea how it was going to unfold. I couldn't have imagined what we would build, how far we would come. I had no idea that we would begin bringing people back into politics in such great numbers.

It started in a single room. My first campaign office was in Montpelier, situated above a chiropractor's office. In the beginning there was one staff person; by the time there were six, we knew we'd outgrown the one-room office with its metal folding chairs and antiquated equipment. I found a larger space in downtown Burlington, in an office I thought was enormous at the time. By winter, even that space was so packed that people were working on top of one another. In May 2003, the office moved to still larger premises.

The staff at Dean for America has been growing almost too quickly to manage. The stories of volunteers with no prior interest in politics showing up on the doorstep have become a cliché, but so many paid staffers did exactly that, starting out as unpaid volunteers.

Apart from the staff, there was an entirely different structure being built outside our supervision. Early in 2003, I learned of a website that organized "meetups"— gatherings of people with similar interests in a particular location. Several hundred people across the country had spontaneously begun to organize on the first Wednesday of every month, talking in coffee shops and restaurants about my campaign for president.

It was clear that the energy of these people had to be harnessed in a positive way, so my staff and I quickly began working to help nurture these independent supporters. At the meetups that I have attended, many of the supporters fit the profile of many of my staff members—they have never been involved politically, but there was something about our campaign that spoke to them. We were seeing a phenomenon where the effort was owned and directed by the people who supported it. In one supporter's phrase, we have made this effort "people-powered."

It is important to remember that I didn't find these people; they found me. The Internet is a tool and it is also a community, linked across the ether. By and large, it is a community that believes America has not lived up to its ideals.

Many of the meetings I've been to this year have been put together largely or entirely on the Internet. This summer, I saw another dramatic demonstration of how the Internet can mobilize grassroots support. Vice President Dick Cheney was holding a $2,000-a-plate fund-raising event in Columbia, South Carolina. I asked my supporters if, over the Internet, they could beat the money-raising efforts of the vice president. And they did. While Vice President Cheney attracted 1,500 people and raised $300,000, 9,621 people contributed to Dean for America and raised $508,640.31.

I believe that the Web is now proving to be a particularly valuable tool for people who care about their communities and who are engaged positively in the political process in the broadest sense. By its nature, the Internet is interactive, a place for discussion and debate and the free exchange of ideas and information. It is entirely different from talk radio, where information generally flows in one direction, from the host to the listener. Radio is interactive only to the extent that the host occasionally might take calls. In my experience, the Internet is a genuine forum for debate. People have talk radio on in the background; they log on to the Internet and *participate*.

People have been responding to my campaign and our message in extraordinary ways. In 2003, several events made it clear to me that I was reaching truly incredible levels of support. The first was a town hall meeting in Seattle on May 14; we filled a space that holds twelve hundred people, and the doors had to be closed. There were people there from the Green Party; there were members of the Machinists Union; there were old-time stalwart Democrats; there were former McCain supporters; and there were even one-time Ross Perot supporters. The surprising thing, however, was those members of the crowd who were none of the above. I stopped in the middle of my speech and said, "Would you raise your hand if you haven't been involved in politics in the last ten or fifteen years?" Half the people in the hall raised their hands. It struck me that these were exactly the types of Americans who have felt excluded from the process, who believed for so long that they had no power to change the course of this country.

This feeling is pervasive. It is clear that Americans are significantly less engaged with politics than they used to be. In 1960, 62.77 percent of the estimated voting age population (VAP)—that is, the number of people who would be eligible to vote—voted in the presidential election. In 2000, that figure had fallen to 51.3 percent. In 1998, just 36.4 percent of the VAP voted in the congressional elections. That means that about half of those eligible to vote in the presidential election did not, along with about two-thirds of those eligible to vote for their member of Congress.

There are further ways of measuring the extent to which Americans are less interested in the political process than they used to be. During the 2000 presidential campaign, the Joan Shorenstein Center on the Press, Politics and Public Policy conducted a study of citizen involvement in the election. (The study was published as a book called *The Vanishing Voter* by Thomas E. Patterson.) We know that fewer Americans are voting, and it turned out that fewer are following the process.

The study showed that, while 60 percent of America's households with televisions watched the presidential debates in 1960, in 2000 that number was less than 30 percent. The study shows that the media itself is less interested in "hard" news and more in "soft" news and "attack journalism." The result was that the 2000 campaign received about half the news coverage of that of 1988's campaign. (In another finding, the center said that 49 percent of poll respondents said it was acceptable for NBC to show a postseason baseball game rather than a presidential debate, against 45 percent who disagreed.)

In the years since 1960, the study points out, America has had more college graduates. Registration is easier and not encumbered by literacy tests, poll taxes, and elaborate registration requirements. Women have been brought fully into the process, and the Motor Voter Act was passed. All of these factors should have produced increased participation, rather than the decline we have witnessed.

I am sure that one of the reasons for this drop in participation is that people have a lower opinion of politicians than they used to. The National Election Studies, Center for Political Studies, at the University of Michigan produces a *Guide to Public Opinion and Electoral Behavior.* Since 1958, they have been asking people how much they trust the federal government. Specifically, the question is, "How much of the time do you think you can trust the government in Washington to do what is right—just about always, most of the time, or only some of the time?" In 2000, 55 percent of respondents said "some of the time"; only 40 percent "most of the time"; and an almost insignificant 4 percent "just about always." In other words, a majority of people do not trust Washington most of the time. In 1964, the figures were 22 percent "some of the time"; 62 percent "most of the time; and 14 percent "just about always," a much more positive set of answers in which more than three-quarters of respondents said they *did* trust Washington most of the time.

In another question, they asked people whether they agreed with the statement "Public officials don't care much what people like me think," and 56 percent agreed, against 33 percent who disagreed. (Ten percent said "neither.") So only a third of respondents positively thought that public officials care about what they think. I think the conclusion we can draw from these results is that many or even most Americans don't trust government and don't think anyone listens to them.

Clearly, Americans are disaffected with politics and with politicians. They do not believe that politicians are responsive to them; they don't think government is on their side; they are not particularly interested in the political process. In the heartland of America, I know there are feelings of antagonism toward government and in some places *politics* is a dirty word. Americans have been turned off by business-as-usual politics, by the slash-and-burn ads that pass for campaigning, by politicians' refusals to give a straight answer to a straight question. This disaffection and lack of trust in the process must be responsible for a significant proportion of the public's lack of engagement. We need people to get involved again.

Part of the answer of how we can reengage people in politics is to speak directly to them. I can't stand Washington speak, the kind of double-talk and evasiveness that is habitual inside the Beltway. I think that most Americans share my aversion.

I talk as simply and directly to people as possible. I think this comes from being a doctor. As far as an individual's health is concerned, you're not doing anyone a favor by not being completely open or honest with them. In medicine, it is incumbent upon the physician to present people with the choices they might have in a way that they can understand. Doctors don't try to talk around an issue, because they can't. As a doctor, I am not allowed to equivocate. It is part of the oath that we take to give a person the best care. Doctors are ethically bound to be candid.

I approach my political life in the same manner that I used when I was a practicing physician. The country, like some patients, faces some choices and some difficult decisions. If a politician doesn't say what the choices are and articulate them simply, he is not doing his job.

I think that this administration and George W. Bush refuse to make it clear to people that there are choices that need to be made and consequences to those decisions. The administration says, "You can have your tax cut, you can have your war in Iraq, and you can have your government programs. You can do all of these things without making any sacrifices or making any choices." This is how we have ended up with a deficit that will likely exceed $500 billion for 2004. The American people know they can't have tax cuts *and* health care; tax cuts *and* education. President Bush has continued to borrow and spend, running up these enormous bills.

That figure of $500 billion takes no longer to write or say than, say, five hundred million. It is difficult to comprehend just how much money $500 billion actually represents. I can put it this way: If I spent $25,000 a day, it would take me 68,493 *years* to spend that much money.

As well as talking clearly, doctors also have to *listen*. A physician will learn a tremendous amount about a patient's health and well-being by listening closely to what the patient has to say. In my time in politics, I've always made it a point to listen to what people have to say to me. I just noted how Americans don't think their politicians care about what they think, and a large part of that might be because they don't think the politicians *listen* to what they are saying.

When I'm on the road, I prefer to stay in people's houses rather than in a hotel. It gives me an opportunity to meet people and hear about their concerns firsthand. I'm reminded of something we used to do each year in Vermont. The legislative session would finish around May 15, and I'd take a trip around the state for a week or so. I'd visit with rotaries, chambers of commerce, and school groups; I'd go into stores and stand on the street and talk to people and listen to what was on their minds. And out of that process my next year's legislative agenda would be distilled.

I'm very grateful for all the kind hospitality—and the terrific home-cooked food—I've had across the country. I recall one visit to a town in Iowa earlier this year. We got in around 11:30 at night, and there was a nice campfire going in the yard of my hosts' house. We sat out for a while, enjoying the pleasant Iowa springtime air, and talked about what life is like in a town of fifteen hundred people. My hosts and their neighbors told me about the strengths and weaknesses of the local economy, about the issues in the schools, and about the excellence of the fishing. The following morning I listened some more over breakfast when some of the neighbors came over.

You can conduct polls and organize focus groups, but nothing beats listening to the real problems of real people. In general, concerns are the same around the country—namely the economy, health care, and education—and each locality also has issues that are particular to it.

I've discovered that Americans are often stronger than Washington thinks, and I've learned a tremendous amount by listening to them. People told me it was clear that educators didn't write the No Child Left Behind bill, and I understood that the people in the Bush administration who put the bill together were ideologues, not educators. By listening to educators, I learned how disastrous this legislation would be.

I think that another reason our democracy is having a difficult time right now is because of the influence of money in our political process. The whole system of lobbyists, special interests, and big money simply turns people off of politics. They watch the process from afar, and they see the special tax breaks and loopholes that special interests are able to obtain, and they understand that our democracy is threatened by a flood of special-interest money pouring into our nation's capital.

Our founders understood that threat. James Madi-son and Thomas Jefferson spoke of their fear that economic power would one day seize political power. And frankly, that fear has been realized with the Bush admin-istration.

Under the Bush administration, the largest corporations and the wealthiest individuals benefit from tax cuts that are bankrupting the states and starving Social Security, Medicare, and our public schools. These tax cuts reward the largest political contributors at the expense of today's middle class, whose property taxes are skyrocketing.

Meanwhile, the oil companies write our energy policy; big pharmaceutical companies draft Medicare reform without price controls; and in Iraq, Halliburton is awarded a $1.7 billion no-bid contract.

It is a government of, by, and for the special interests. The only way the American people are included in the process is that we are left to pay the bills. And the cost is high—to our economy, our environment, our children's schools, and our health care.

I almost always close my stump speech by reminding people of Abraham Lincoln's immortal phrase from the Gettysburg Address: "Government of the people, by the people, for the people." As a country, we are as committed to that ideal as ever, but somewhere along the way, we have lost the goodwill and interest of many of the people themselves.

Those of us who see the government as a force for good in society face a daunting challenge. We need to reengage people in the political process so that the health of our democracy is maintained. We need to encourage the 50 percent of the population that does not vote to participate.

I've learned a great deal as I've traveled around the country. I know that we need to challenge the notion that people cannot listen to straight talk, and I know we need to lessen the influence of big money. I think these are ways by which Americans can become involved in politics again.

As I've gone around America, many of the people I've met have been disengaged from politics, and now we're seeing them getting involved. In some cases, these people were politically active in the past but stopped being involved for one reason or another. In many other instances, these were people who had never really been interested in politics before. Perhaps they didn't think that politicians had anything to say to them. Remember, almost 50 percent of Americans did not even vote at the last election, so there are millions and millions of people I hope can be introduced, or reintroduced, to the political process. One of the ways I think that can be done is by replacing negative ads, attacks, cynicism, and desperation with a positive vision of America for all Americans, not just the rich and not just the special interests.

I have also seen large numbers of Democrats who have

watched their party drift away from them in recent years getting involved again. The party has undoubtedly moved to the right in recent years as it has followed the focus of the political debate. This means that the choices the party is offering have moved to the right, as well. A significant part of the core Democratic constituency has been left behind and become stranded as a result. I believe that this is an important reason why Democrats have not been successful in recent years: As a party, we have ignored our base and not given the voters a reason to go to the polls.

At the same time, the Republican Party has molded the debate and set the agenda. The Republicans have succeeded in getting their core supporters fired up, and they are coming out to the polls. Swing voters are also voting because that is where the parties have gone hunting for votes. The only people left whose views are not being adequately represented are voters who have traditionally supported the Democratic Party, and I believe we have no one to blame for that but ourselves.

These Democrats believe deeply in the core values of the party, and they believe the party isn't standing up for them. If the party stands up for what we believe and offers a coherent alternative to the policies of the current administration, we will engage more and more people, and reengage more and more people, in the political process.

I have seen these people turning up in large numbers to events as I've moved around America.

On June 9, 2003, we held a rally in East Austin, Texas, a town populated largely by Latino Americans. I expected a crowd of three hundred. Thirty-two hundred people showed up, and I was stunned. A few volunteers had worked for six days straight. They did everything online or over the phone, never mailing a letter. It has been very common to have crowds that are two, three, or four times larger than I expected, but for a crowd to be ten times larger was beyond belief.

At the California state Democratic convention in Sacramento in March, I gave a "red meat" speech about hope, community, and health care. Some people were weeping and others were jumping up and down. People wrote $10 and $25 checks and threw them at Dean staffers.

In August, I went on the "Sleepless Summer Tour," ten stops in eight states in four days. At an early stop, I started talking to a crowd in Spokane, Washington. The gathering seemed about the size I'd been told to expect, maybe two hundred people. I started in on my speech but right away I was told to stop. Apparently I wasn't talking to the main rally; this was just the overflow crowd that couldn't fit in the room anymore.

There were still more people on other stops: 5,000 in Portland, 10,000 in Seattle. I was astonished at every turn. In Chicago, 3,500 people came out on an extremely hot day. I talked to the crowd, and five minutes after I finished speaking, the heavens opened up and it poured rain.

If it had rained during the speech, of course I'd have dealt with it. I have come to expect the unexpected. I remember an event at Luther College in Decorah, Iowa, when a fire alarm went off and we had to evacuate the building. The meeting was going extremely well, so well that someone suggested a Republican set off the alarm. But we were able to regroup and gather on a lawn at the college, and the event only got better. On a beautiful day, a crowd of 75 grew into a crowd of 120, and I kept talking to people an hour longer than we planned.

In New York this summer, at the last stop on the Sleepless Summer Tour, I spoke to another huge gathering, this one at Bryant Park. It is an extraordinary feeling to be standing up in front of over ten thousand people, feeling their energy and excitement and feeding off of it. I went home to Burlington after that event and got in around 1:30 in the morning. (That really was a sleepless tour.) I remember thinking back a year, to the office in the small room above the chiropractor's office in Montpelier, where this all began.

When I give a speech, unless it is a major policy announcement, I don't use a prepared text. Sometimes, perhaps, I should, but generally I decide what to talk about once I'm at the podium and can gauge the crowd. I often find, particularly with larger audiences, that this allows me to reflect the enormous energy and hope of the crowd. This is a very powerful sensation. When you are reflecting the energy of 4,000 or 10,000 people back at them, you get an extraordinary result.

I know in my heart that it's not me the crowds on the road are responding to, it's not some brilliant insight that I'm bringing to them. The crowds are so energized because for the first time in years they're hearing someone say what they believe—and in a way that nobody else dares to do. This movement we're creating certainly isn't about me. When I go home I'm just an ordinary person who likes to putter around in old clothes and take out the trash. This movement is about the people taking back their country, and in reality I am following the people's lead.

I think I also reflect back the optimism that people have about what this country can be, the country they want to be a part of. Across America, we are drawing people together in a way that hasn't happened in far too long. Many of them have not participated in a campaign for many years, if ever, because they have been disillusioned with politicians and the political process. Many are from disenfranchised communities who have not seen a reason to vote before because they haven't thought their vote will make a difference. Many feel powerless in the face of an unresponsive government. Many are young and many are young at heart; many are African-American and many are Asian-American, Native American, and many are Latino. But all are yearning to reconnect with one another in a community for all Americans.

The level of enthusiasm on the Sleepless Summer Tour surpassed any I had ever seen, and it was incredible to me that what had begun as such a small effort had experienced such tremendous growth.

I don't begin to take personal credit for the reaction any of the people have had. I happen to believe that there was a deeper sentiment that I had spoken to, but I did not create the depth of that sentiment. It has gradually become clear to me that there exists a tremendous loss of hope among so many Americans, a feeling of powerlessness that this country has not seen for many, many years. The idea that the people do in fact have the power to change history and change their country is filling many Americans with hope again.

The hope is beginning to spread in unexpected ways. I heard from a young woman in Pennsylvania who sold her bicycle so she could use the money to contribute to the campaign. Her words were: "I sold my bicycle for democracy."

Earlier this year, some of my supporters wrote personal letters to citizens in Iowa and New Hampshire, explaining why they were supporting the campaign. The results were phenomenal; through a simple letter-writing effort, Americans from entirely different parts of the country were brought together.

One of the letters happened to go to Jim Autry, the husband of Sally Pederson, the lieutenant governor of Iowa. I called Jim and he read me the letter. The meetup volunteer from California who had written the letter said she was afraid the country had lost its spirituality. She said there was no acknowledgment by the leadership of the country that this was a community, no acknowledgment that we are all one people. The woman desperately wanted us to be one family again, inspired as we once were under the direction of leaders like John F. Kennedy.

One supporter, Max Philby, wrote the following message about the campaign, which has become so much larger than me: "I know now, here in this moment, that we can do this. It's going to be the most intense fifteen months in American politics in three decades. But we can do this. And as Americans, we are called to do this. We are called to serve our nation as patriots of this country. We are called to restore honor and meaning to our flag, to our communities and to our standing in the world. And we can do this. All that it takes is all that we have to give to it."

I have come to believe that a true grassroots campaign— a campaign really of the people, by the people, and for the people—can take this country back. With hundreds of thousands of supporters like Max Philby, each reaching out in their communities to neighbors and friends, we can fight back against the special interests. Hundreds of thousands of people at the grass roots, meeting up and organizing, putting out flyers and knocking on doors.

And while the president is amassing a war chest bundled in $100,000 and $200,000 increments by those he calls "Rangers" and "Pioneers," Americans from across the country will match that and fight against it with their $50 contributions.

What we are doing is nothing less than shifting the balance of power in politics back to the American people. I believe that this will be the greatest grassroots campaign in the history of American politics and that this election will truly be remembered as a watershed when the American democracy was restored to its rightful owners, the American people.

CHAPTER

★ 14 ★

Vermont has a strong sense of community, and my family has been fortunate to be a part of it. It's the sort of place where one week you can disagree with your neighbor at a town meeting over spending money to hire an additional gym coach, and the next you have some trouble and that same neighbor is at your door with a covered dish, offering whatever help you might need.

Community has been rooted in Vermont culture for as long as people have lived here. The town meeting, for example, is a tradition that predates the founding of Vermont in 1777. Once a year, all the town residents who were eligible to vote would get together and decide how much they'd be taxed and how the money would be spent. For many years, Vermont was governed this way at the local level.

Town meetings are still held in Vermont to this day. In

fact, many of the smaller towns have meetings in which people can, for instance, amend the school budget right from the floor. The tradition allows people to vote on whether to buy a new grader for the road, whether to borrow money, and what the tax rate should be. Usually the meeting is an all-day affair, and town meeting day is a state holiday. Everyone gets to know their neighbors, and people generally bring something to eat, so they can break bread together and share their ideas informally. If you have a school budget to set, you're not going to leave the meeting without fixing that budget. If it doesn't pass the first time, you change it so it does pass. Town meetings represent democracy at its most basic level, and they encourage a culture of citizen and community participation.

When I was governor, I would go to a number of town meetings—four or five on a Tuesday and others in some towns who had moved the meetings to the previous night so that working people could attend. I would watch as the people of Vermont came together to cooperate in the best interests of the entire community.

I fear that the sense of community we have in Vermont at our town meetings has been lost in the country as a whole, and I believe this breakdown of community and participation has been encouraged and abetted by a president who divides us against one another in service of his ideology.

The longer I spend on the road, the more aware I become of the decline of community in America and the clearer it becomes that the work of rebuilding our American community cannot wait. There is so much work to be done to change America. That's why I'm so proud of an idea my supporters in Iowa came up with, which they've called Dean Corps, to rebuild their local communities.

Dean Corps is based on AmeriCorps. Members devote their time, energy, and labor to community service. Dean Corps began in Iowa, intending to fill the vacuum left by the Bush administration's underfunding of AmeriCorps, which hit Iowa particularly hard. Dean Corps has been active in the unemployed community in Iowa, and it is also doing environmental outreach and developing programs to help ensure that the needs of seniors are met.

The first Dean Corps event I participated in was at the Johnson County Crisis Center in Iowa City. We bagged groceries for unemployed Iowans who were having difficulty making ends meet. After the event, Dean Corps volunteers collected more than 320 pounds of donated food to replenish the stocks.

The Johnson County Crisis Center also hosts a crisis phone line, provides transient services, and distributes clothing. The need is great; demand at the food bank has increased 35 percent recently due to the terrible economic climate. Currently, more than half of its clients are unemployed, up from 38 percent last year.

The crisis center exists because hardworking Americans are willing to volunteer their time. Thanks to the contribution of these Iowans, their neighbors have a resource to fall back on when they are having trouble feeding their families. In Johnson County, residents contribute $700,000 a year in donated goods and volunteer hours to help run the center's programs.

The Johnson County Crisis Center stands on the front lines of the Bush economy. People at the center have a first-hand glimpse at problems caused by the Bush tax cuts and the Bush administration's record federal deficits; they do not need statistics to see that states are now being forced to cut their services and raise taxes. These local volunteers understand what it means to have higher property taxes and fewer jobs, fewer police officers and firefighters, fewer teachers and larger classes. Fiscal irresponsibility is not just an academic concept; it has real consequences for working families, in Iowa and all across America.

Since President Bush took office, two thousand manufacturing jobs have been lost in southeast Iowa. The unemployment rate stands at 6 percent, and in 2001, Iowa bankruptcy filings reached an all-time high of 11,074—increasing by almost 34 percent from the year before.

The Bush administration's policies have left states like Iowa ill-prepared to deal with the effects of this economy—there are fewer resources for people out of work, fewer options for the unemployed, and less government support for places like the crisis center. President Bush chose tax cuts over funding teachers and education, he chose tax cuts over funding AmeriCorps, he chose tax cuts over expanding health care, and he chose tax cuts over funding homeland security. Each time the choice was made, the consequences were felt in our communities.

• • •

Diversity is part of the strength of the American community and it needs to be nurtured. Extraordinary demographic change is sweeping the United States, and by midcentury, if not before, white people will no longer constitute a majority of the population. This threshold is already being crossed by an ever-larger number of institutions, communities, and states.

Our economic and social success in the twenty-first century depend on overcoming the persistent racial disparities that divide us. The current administration has neither acknowledged nor confronted this challenge. Instead, their divisiveness has contributed to the breakdown of our national community. They have divided us by race, and the bipartisan national consensus on civil rights that has led to such important advances over the last fifty years has begun to unravel in the first three years of the Bush presidency.

For example, there is hard-core unemployment in minority communities. The Bureau of Labor Statistics reports that the overall unemployment rate in August 2003 was 6.1 percent, but among African-Americans it was 10.9 percent and among Hispanics, 7.8 percent. Even during the economic boom of the late 1990s, the unemployment rates for African-Americans and Hispanics were 10.3 percent and 7.4 percent, respectively, while the unemployment rate for whites was 4.0 percent. Worse, *The Wall Street Journal* recently published a study showing that white job applicants with drug convictions were more likely to be called back for a second interview than were African-American applicants with clean records.

There are significant disparities in rates of poverty. According to the 2000 census, 11.3 percent of all Americans live below the poverty line, but 22.1 percent of African-Americans do—this is three times as large as the 7.5 percent poverty rate for whites. In rural areas, minority poverty rates are especially dramatic: 31.4 percent of African-Americans living outside of cities were below the poverty line, compared with 25 percent of nonurban Hispanics and 11.1 percent of nonurban whites.

The National Institutes of Health has identified disparities between minorities and other Americans in the incidence of cancer, diabetes, infant mortality, AIDS, cardiovascular illnesses, and many other diseases. Part of the problem is access to health insurance. Other factors include differences in environmental and occupational exposures to hazardous chemicals, since minorities are more likely to live in polluted environments and to work in dangerous occupations.

Racial inequality in the criminal justice system is longstanding and growing. Minorities are victimized by well-documented racial profiling, by racially skewed charging and plea bargaining decisions, and by harsh mandatory sentencing laws. As a result, on any given day almost one in three African-American males between the ages of twenty and twenty-nine is under some form of criminal supervision—either in prison or jail, or on probation or parole. An African-American male born in 1991 has a one in three chance of spending time in prison at some point in his life. A Hispanic male born in 1991 has a one in six chance of spending time in prison.

Incredibly, there are now more young African-American men under criminal supervision than there are in college. For every one African-American male who graduates from college, one hundred are arrested.

There are also grave racial disparities in the application of the death penalty. I believe capital punishment should be available in especially heinous cases like the Oklahoma City bombing, but it must always be carried out in a fair and reliable manner. Attorney General Janet Reno tried to root out racial and geographic disparity in the federal death penalty, but Attorney General John Ashcroft has reversed course. His Justice Department has been three times more likely to seek the death penalty for African-American defendants accused of killing white victims than for African-Americans accused of killing nonwhites, according to the Federal Death Penalty Resource Counsel Project.

At the same time, the Bush/Ashcroft Justice Department has undermined efforts to redress racial disparities in federal drug sentencing laws. Current law mandates the same five-year prison term for a defendant convicted of selling 500 grams of powder cocaine and a defendant convicted of selling only 5 grams of crack cocaine. There is no scientific evidence to justify treating crack cocaine as though it were one hundred times more dangerous than powder cocaine, yet the effect of the ratio is a skyrocketing minority incarceration rate because almost all federal crack defendants— 93.7 percent in 2000—are African-American or Hispanic.

There are plenty of white crack users and dealers, but they don't get charged under these unfair federal laws.

The independent U.S. Sentencing Commission has endorsed sensible reforms. But the Bush administration has endorsed the 100-to-1 disparity in current law, describing the current penalty structure as "proper."

I was outraged when President Bush used the inflammatory word *quota* to describe the University of Michigan program, and I criticized him for distorting the facts. Fortunately the Supreme Court rejected that misleading label. I think it is a gross disservice to the public and to the solemn obligation of leadership on matters of race when the president uses this word. The use of the word *quota* is a deliberate appeal to the fears of whites that minorities will take their jobs and places in institutions of higher learning. The business of race is too important and too sensitive— distortions like this will only fuel misunderstanding, resentment, and distrust. Playing this kind of political race card reflects monstrous cynicism. Affirmative action remains a vitally important tool in a number of settings to combat discrimination and remedy its lingering effects.

Affirmative action in education is especially important. First, as the Supreme Court recognized, the promotion of diversity is a legitimate and valuable goal. Second, affirmative action helps to address the widely recognized achievement gap between minority students and nonminority students, directly related to income levels and the quality of schools in many minority neighborhoods. Average reading and math scores for African-American and Hispanic students are consistently lower than the scores of white students. According to the widely respected Education Trust, minority students in twelfth grade are, on average, about four years behind other young people in reading and other skills. African-American and Hispanic high school students are statistically more likely to drop out of school in every state, and, of all high school graduates, fewer African-Americans and Hispanics than whites attend college. Closing the education achievement gap requires federal resources, but the Bush administration offers hollow rhetoric instead.

We have made great progress since the days of Jim Crow, and public attitudes on race have undergone dramatic changes. But white Americans believe that racism is not much of a problem anymore, and African-American and Latino Americans interpret indifference and insensitivity on the part of white Americans as racism. And, in fact, indifference in hiring leads to institutional bias. That is why the Bush administration is wrong to attack affirmative action. The Bush folks pander to our biases instead of speaking out against them.

Discrimination persists and we continue to be divided by race. Despite the landmark civil rights laws of the 1960s, many neighborhoods and school systems remain segregated. We are a long way from the society Martin Luther King, Jr., dreamed about, one in which children are judged by the content of their character rather than the color of their skin. Civil rights remains the unfinished business of America.

• • •

Immigrants are vital to this country. When I am giving a speech, I will often stop and ask how many people in the audience are Native American. A couple of people might put up their hands. Then I say, "The rest of you are all immigrants, the sons and daughters and grandchildren and descendants of immigrants." This is the legacy of our country.

Today, immigrants are among the hardest-working people in this country. They're often working two jobs, paying their taxes, and contributing to the well-being of their community. They came here for a better life and are looking to raise their kids and give them in turn a better life than they had themselves. This aspiration and hard work are part of the strength of our nation, and we need to support these hard-working people. We cannot allow politicians to try to divide us and turn us against them on the basis of their being immigrants or on the basis of race.

The president has also divided us by gender, attacking reproductive choice and attempting to deny women the right to make their own medical decisions.

As a physician, I have a different perspective from many politicians on the issue of a woman's right to choose. I believe that the issue of abortion is a medical rather than a political decision. I don't see how a government regulation that tells doctors how to practice medicine can be supported. Republicans claim they are the party of individual freedom, but they are the first to tell other people how to live their lives.

A pregnant woman can be faced with a very difficult choice. She can give up a child for adoption. In that case, there will always be a part of her that wonders what would have happened if she had done things differently. She can decide to have the baby, and her life—particularly if she is an unmarried mother—will change dramatically. She might have to give up her education, her job, and even her well-being. If she is a teenager, she stands a good chance of ending up on welfare or she can have an abortion.

Whatever she decides to do, it is the woman who is going to have to live with the consequences for the rest of her life. It seems to me that it is her choice to make. It is not President Bush's choice. It is not the choice of any member of Congress. Abortion is a matter between the physician and the patient, and I do not believe it is any of the government's business. That's why I am pro-choice.

I am against the gag rule in any form. It is something that ethically no doctor should ever support. For politicians to dictate what doctors can tell a patient is wrong and should be offensive to any physician. Essentially, the gag rule dictates what a doctor can and cannot say about family planning to his or her patients.

In 1988, the Reagan administration forbade Title X clinics from providing advice about abortion and from offering referrals. (Title X refers to a 1970 law that established federally funded family planning clinics.) This was the original gag rule. The ruling was never implemented in the United States, and in 1993, the Clinton administration rescinded it.

On January 22, 2001—the twenty-eighth anniversary of the landmark *Roe v. Wade* decision—President Bush announced he would withhold federal money going to organizations abroad that supported legal abortion. This is a global gag rule that goes so far as to stop organizations from using their own money to provide abortion services or advocate for abortion rights. The gag rule is a favorite Republican device originated under the Reagan administration, supported by George H. W. Bush and brandished by the right wing in Congress who succeeded in attaching one to a foreign appropriations bill in 1999.

This administration has a bad record in many areas of particular concern to women. President Bush has even admitted the possibility of a challenge to *Roe v. Wade*. This is how an editorial in *The New York Times* summarized the administration's stance:

> The lengthening string of anti-choice executive orders, regulations, legal briefs, legislative maneuvers, and key appointments emanating from his administration suggests that undermining the reproductive freedom essential to women's health, privacy, and equality is a major preoccupation of his administration—second only, perhaps, to the war on terrorism.

The administration is undermining American women in so many ways.

In his 2003 budget, President Bush increased funding for abstinence-only sex education to $135 million, a 30 percent increase. Jody Ratner of the Center for Reproductive Rights said, "Under the pretext of preventing teen pregnancy, the Bush administration's abstinence-only focus harms teenagers by denying them critical, potentially life-saving information about contraception, safer sex practices, and sexuality."

Women still earn less for doing the same job as a man in America. Women earn about 72 percent of what men do for similar jobs, which represents an average loss of $4,229 per year. Diana Furchtgott-Roth, a former member of President Bush's Council of Economic Advisers, has said, "It's simply false that in an ideal world men and women would have equal incomes." Clearly, pay equity is of no interest to this administration. In fact, the administration closed down the program in the Department of Labor that was supposed to enforce pay equity.

I am a firm believer in Title IX, the federal law that barred sexual discrimination against women and girls in athletics. I believe that my daughter should have the same opportunities in sports that my son had. In June 2002, Secretary of Education Roderick Paige created the Commission on Opportunity in Athletics to review Title IX and, in January 2003, made recommendations that would ease the regulations of Title IX, which, if enacted, would reduce opportunities for women and girls in sports.

And in his 2004 budget, President Bush proposed large cuts to several Department of Justice grant programs—including programs under the Violence Against Women

Act. Senator Joe Biden, who sponsored the Violence Against Women Act, said, "I find it ironic that the very agency charged with enforcing the laws and protecting women is willfully ignoring the law and hindering efforts to prevent violence against women."

The president has accused the Democrats of class warfare, when it is the president himself who has waged class warfare by further dividing Americans by income. He has focused his tax cuts on those people who are likely to support Republican candidates, while cutting veterans' health benefits and children's health care, and he is standing by as more than 41 million Americans suffer from a lack of health insurance.

American working families are working harder and harder and getting less and less. Americans I have met have told me that they are having a tougher time making ends meet. The American dream has always been about opportunity; that we would work hard today to give the next generation a better future. That dream is becoming harder and harder to realize.

Married couples now work ten weeks longer a year than they did in 1968. Today, a family with two workers who both work full-time is taking in less net income than a family with one member working a generation ago. And they have to do more with that money. They have to worry about health care; they have to worry about retirement at the same time that they have to bear more and more of the tax burden in this country while the wealthy and corporations are bearing less and less.

There are four basic areas of support for working families: health care, help with the kids, retirement, and tax relief. President Bush is not working toward universal health care. It is unacceptable that 41 million Americans do not have any health insurance. The United States is the only industrialized nation in the world that doesn't have health insurance for all its citizens. We are lagging behind many nations: the United Kingdom, France, Germany, Canada, Israel, Japan. There is universal health care in Costa Rica, but not in the United States.

I have always believed that universal health care is a practical necessity for the citizens of this country, and we worked to try to implement it for the people of Vermont. The clarion call for full coverage has long been heard in our party. As long ago as 1948, Harry S. Truman said, "Millions of our citizens do not now have a full measure of opportunity to achieve and enjoy good health. Millions do not now have protection or security against the economic effects of sickness. The time has arrived for action to help them attain that opportunity and that protection."

Not only are we not making progress toward universal health care but the president is cutting existing programs, slashing funding for Medicaid and the State Children's Health Insurance Program by $2.5 billion.

All parents struggle with how to take care of their children before they go to school. Then they worry whether the schools will be good enough, and then they worry whether they will be able to afford college. We are obliged to help families in these areas, but these are areas President Bush has cut: He has cut assistance to higher education, he's cut assistance in child care, he's cut assistance to Head Start by looking to block grant it. Head Start has a thirty-eight-year record of success, and it should not be dismantled.

I was as happy as anyone when President Bush made education reform a priority for his administration. But the president's 2001 education bill, No Child Left Behind (NCLB)—or No Schoolboard Left Standing, as I prefer to think of it—is a disaster. George W. Bush wanted to be the education president, but he has done more to harm education than any president in my memory.

NCLB is the second-largest unfunded mandate in the history of education in this country. That means that the federal government requires the states to institute change without Washington paying for it. This is causing huge increases in property taxes across the country.

One of the few regrets I have about not running for a sixth term for governor is that, had I run and been re-elected, we would have refused the money from No Child Left Behind. I believe the state would have been better off without the small amount of money and still being able to run our own school system.

There was one really important step forward in this act, and we can't lose sight of that: the recognition that success in a school needs to include all the children, in particular, groups that might be minorities within the student body. When you look at the school as a whole and say it's succeeding on average, that can mask some very real gaps facing disadvantaged kids. As we look to fix No Child Left Behind, that's one principle I'd like to keep.

NCLB is a disaster. The imposition on the rest of the country by George W. Bush of the failing educational model that they have in Texas means that education in most states is going to get worse. NCLB identifies schools that are doing very well as failing; it mandates transportation expenses without paying for them; it requires qualifications for teachers without having any way to pay the extra money for those qualifications. And all it does is encourage states to reduce their standards in a disastrous race to the bottom, what I view as the dumbing down of the American school system. Ohio reduced the number of schools that "failed" under the provisions of NCLB from 760 to 212 by reducing its standards. Somehow, NCLB rates one-third of all schools in Michigan as failing, but none at all in Arkansas and Wyoming. It is difficult to believe that a third of all schools in one state are worse than every one of the schools in any other.

Besides health care and education, every American worker should have some security about their retirement. Through Social Security and Medicare, government has played a tremendously important role in providing that security to our seniors. Hardworking Americans deserve to know that when they retire they will have a certain level of income and of medical care guaranteed. That is why these programs are such an essential part of our country and such a great legacy from the New Deal and the Great Society. They represent the best of government.

I will never allow the Republicans to destroy these two

great programs. Their attempts to privatize Social Security or to provide Medicare in vouchers have to be defeated. Sure, both of these programs are going to present very difficult financial challenges to American society as the baby boomers begin to retire in 2010. But we have faced these problems before, and with bipartisan cooperation and real national leadership, we have addressed them—and we will again. We have the ability to meet our obligations as a community to our parents and our elderly neighbors. They built the country we know and love today. We have an obligation to ensure that none of them ends up in poverty or in need of medical assistance that they just can't afford. I am pretty sure the American people are willing to do what it takes to fulfill that obligation.

The fourth area where I think government has to help working families is with tax relief. Corporate America used to carry a lot more of the burden of American society than they do today. Today, that burden is falling on the shoulders of working people and their families. In the 1950s, corporations paid 39 percent of taxes, individuals 61 percent. Today, corporations pay 17 percent of taxes and everyone else pays 83 percent. I have seen figures that show that, in 2001, the corporate share of taxes paid was down to 13 percent.

And most of this is because the tax code has been taken over by corporate welfare and corporate loopholes to the tune of $150 billion a year by some estimates. Even more disturbing to me is the number of people who don't pay what they actually owe. According to a former commissioner of the Internal Revenue Service, tax cheats owe about $30 billion in taxes, and they are getting away with it because the IRS doesn't have the resources—the people or the computers—to collect it.

So it's clear that the tax burden in this country has shifted to the people, but not to all the people. The highest income tax rates have been cut dramatically. From the end of the Second World War until the rates were reduced under the Kennedy administration, the highest rate was 91 percent. By 2006, the highest rate will be 35 percent. In a study whose preliminary results were released in August 2003, Professor Emmanuel Saez of Berkeley says we now have "a much flatter tax structure where an upper middle class family will face the same marginal tax rate as the richest income earners in the United States."

What the Bush administration is doing is trying to shift the tax load in this country from wealth to labor. Wealth is generated in three ways without working. One is capital gains from owning stocks or owning a business that appreciates and proceeds are taken when it is sold. The second is dividends on shares. The third is estates. These are the precise income sources this administration is removing tax from: everything that you don't have to work for. Meanwhile, the working family is carrying more of the burden.

President Bush's tax cuts in 2001 and 2003 disproportionately helped people who did not need help. The Tax Policy Center estimates that 42 percent of the money given back in the 2001 cut will go to the top 1 percent of earning families (those making more than $330,000 a year). The 2003 cut actually concentrates 17.3 percent of its bounty on the top 0.13 percent (just over one in a thousand), those families making more than $1 million a year. They are getting more help than the bottom 70 percent of American families. In real terms, for most families, the tax cut is of little help. If you make more than a million dollars a year, you will do fine; the real cut for families in the middle of the income distribution in 2002 was $469.

The president financed his tax cut by taking money out of Social Security and taking health care benefits away from veterans. The men and women he sent to Afghanistan and to Iraq are going to come back to fewer benefits and are going to have to pay off our enormous national debt. The president's tax cuts have saddled future generations with debt. Since George W. Bush came to office, the federal debt has grown by over $1 trillion. We've gone from having nearly a $5 trillion surplus over ten years to a nearly $3 trillion deficit over the same period. That's an $8 trillion swing—a number that is nearly impossible to get one's mind around. Try this: One trillion dollars is more than 3,400 for every American man, woman, and child. So for every single American, this swing represents a loss of $28,000, to be paid off with interest over the coming generation. Sure, the president was proud to say he got rid of the so-called death tax, but what he really did was to pass on the biggest inheritance tax in the history of the country.

Warren Buffett wrote an op-ed in *The Washington Post* about the tax cut on dividends. Buffett is the CEO of Berkshire Hathaway, which doesn't pay a dividend. If the company decided to pay a $1 billion dividend in 2004, Buffett, who owns 31 percent of the company, would theoretically receive $310 million and it would be tax free. Currently, he pays about the same proportion of his income in tax—about 30 percent—as the receptionist in his office. This huge windfall would mean that his real tax rate fell to 3 percent while the company's receptionist would still be paying 30 percent, ten times his rate.

Buffett said he thought that giving 310,000 families $1,000 each would probably do more to stimulate the economy than giving Buffett $310 million. The fact that the president's tax cuts benefit only the wealthy demonstrates how he has abandoned the American middle class. As Buffett points out, giving a break to one class of taxpayer—in this case, what he describes as that "nonendangered species," the rich—means that somewhere, either now or in the future, someone else has to pick up the tab.

There are areas of our economy that require immediate attention and that are being ignored. Our infrastructure is one. At a time when the president has gone to Congress to ask for $87 billion to help rebuild Iraq, the American Society of Civil Engineers issued a report on the American infrastructure. Our school buildings were given a grade of D–, our roads a D+. There are twenty-six hundred unsafe dams in the country, and a quarter of the bridges are in bad repair.

Instead of the reckless economic agenda this administration has pursued, I believe we need to focus on creating jobs, balancing the budget, and ensuring that working Americans and their families can make ends meet. To create jobs, we've got to invest again, not just in infrastructure but in the research and development of the industries that will propel this country to the future from technology to broadband to biotech. And we need a special focus on small business, which is the single biggest engine of job creation. Small businesses stay in their communities, they don't move overseas.

But all of this is unlikely under an administration that divides us by income and doesn't truly have in its heart the interests of middle-class working Americans. We can really only truly restore our sense of American community when every American family feels it has economic opportunity and economic security. And that won't happen so long as economic and tax policy is created for the benefit of large donors to the Republican Party.

Finally, President Bush has also divided our American community by sexual orientation, refusing to condemn both Senator Rick Santorum and Justice Antonin Scalia after each made bigoted remarks about homosexuals.

In 2000, when I was still governor, Vermont made history by becoming the first state to sanction civil unions between same-sex couples. The civil unions battle demonstrates my absolute commitment to civil rights and equality under the law. It also shows that I'm not about to be bullied when I have set my mind to something. The depth of hate and prejudice shown by antigay forces made me determined to see it through, whatever the political cost might be.

In 1999, three Vermont same-sex couples sued the state after they were denied marriage licenses. The Vermont

Supreme Court ruled that gay and lesbian couples were being denied the same legal rights as heterosexual couples.

This was an election year, and I knew there would be a serious furor. When the bill first appeared, there was a suggestion that we could appoint a commission that would study the legislation for a year or so. That wasn't something I was prepared to contemplate. We weren't going to tell gay people they could remain second-class citizens another year, while legislators and the governor got themselves re-elected. Compromise is something to consider when you are managing a budget, not when it comes to fundamental human rights.

An hour and a half after the decision came down from the supreme court, I said that we were going to support domestic partner legislation. The bill gave gay and lesbian people who undertook the legal commitment of a civil union the same rights—financial, inheritance, hospital visitation, and insurance rights—as married heterosexual couples. At the same time, they also assumed the same obligations.

One of the most important roles of a governor is to provide leadership, and I believe this was my biggest contribution to civil unions. I didn't have to do a lot of lobbying—there were a few people I spoke to who were wavering. But when the legislature saw I was going to support the bill, it helped strengthen the will of those lawmakers who knew they should support it, too.

In the state, there was an outpouring of protest against the legislation. Supporters of the bill were abused in public.

Our office was inundated with hate-filled calls and threats, and we were accused of teaching homosexuality in schools. As I went around the state discussing the issue, I was even advised to wear a bulletproof vest at some events. I know that as far as I was concerned, the worse the attacks became, the more determined I was that I would try to ensure the legislation would pass.

Of course, some people thought civil unions didn't go far enough and that we should have proposed gay marriage. I think churches should decide who gets married and who doesn't. The civil and legal aspects are the responsibility of the legislature. Thanks to civil unions, gay and lesbian couples have the same legal rights as heterosexuals, which is the heart of the matter.

I saw firsthand the courage displayed by some legislators who voted for the bill. It was a very emotional issue, and I deeply admired some individuals who voted the right way, even though they lost their seats as a result.

On April 25, 2000, Vermont legislators passed HB847, as it was designated, and I signed it into law. The new Civil Unions Law went into effect on July 1. We didn't have a bill-signing ceremony, which was somewhat controversial. Signing ceremonies are by their nature a gesture of triumph. There were decent people who opposed the measure, and I thought we'd have to win them over by being thoughtful and listening to their point of view. Because of their support of civil unions, sixteen incumbents in the house—eleven Democrats, four Republicans, and one independent—lost their seats, and the house went Republican. We had some polling numbers in the early days of the civil unions fight that showed we had only 30 percent support for the measure. In the end, I was fortunate to be able to overcome that opposition in my race and won reelection by the same margin as in previous years. That taught me that if you stand up for what you believe, you can still win an election even if the voters disagree with you.

Vermonters have become used to the idea of civil unions. They realize that equal justice for all doesn't mean less justice for anybody. At the moment, Vermont is the only state that has equal rights under the law for every human being. Justices of the peace who perform the ceremony have told me how extraordinary these unions are. Two people who love each other, who have been persecuted in other states, come to Vermont and are able to set off on a life together just as any other couple would.

If you fall in love with somebody who happens to be the same sex, you have many fewer rights in this country. Gay people are the last group against whom it is legal to discriminate. I hope that the fight for civil unions in Vermont is the beginning of the end for discrimination against any American.

I believe that all people are created equal, certainly in the eyes of God. Therefore, they should be equal in the eyes of the law. That's why I knew I had to work for civil unions. I never viewed the bill as a gay rights issue. I signed it out of a commitment to human rights, and because every single American has the same right to equality and justice under the law that I have.

During this campaign, I gave a speech in Washington, D.C., and afterward, a gentleman who must have been eighty years old came up to me. He said, "I want to thank you for signing the Civil Unions bill." I was a little taken aback. I'd been speaking to a Democratic audience rather than a specifically gay one, and I don't normally think of most seniors as having an interest in civil unions. I was very curious as to why this man was interested.

What he told me was that he'd been on the beach at Normandy on D-day in 1944, and comrades of his had been killed all around him. As he told me, "I'm gay," it brought home a realization that maybe should have been obvious to me all along. Americans who happen to be gay have been serving their country with extraordinary bravery under horrendous circumstances. Some have been braver in the service of their country than the vast majority of Americans who condemned gay rights would ever dare to be. It seems to me that someone who is willing to serve and die for his country is someone who deserves the same rights as everyone else in America.

I am tired of our country being divided by race, by economic status, by gender, and by sexual orientation. This is not the America we were taught to believe in. There is so much that we can accomplish if we are united as one national community. I believe we deserve leadership that will appeal to the best in our natures, rather than pandering to the worst in us, and George W. Bush has been the most divisive president this country has seen since Richard Nixon.

I am not alone. The Americans I have met love their country. They want to see it united again. They are tired of leadership that blames the problems of America on one group or another, be it low-income people, minorities, gays and lesbians, disabled people, women, immigrants, or any other easily scapegoated "them." As President Clinton said upon accepting the Democratic nomination in 1992, this is America. There is no them; there is only us.

We need to re-create the sense of community in this country. It is not just about ending the divisions that George W. Bush and the Republicans are causing; it is also about creating that sense of community again.

Together, we can build an America where it is important not only that my family has health care but that my neighbor's family has health care, as well. We can build an America where it is important not only that my children receive a quality education but that my neighbor's children are educated, as well. We can build an America not only where I have equal rights and security and a job to go to each day but where we ensure that every American is safe, every American is working, and every American is equal under the law.

The spirit of community that is so strong in Vermont was once alive in every corner of America. It can be so again. I believe that in cities and towns across the country, through groups like Dean Corps and through the outreach of citizens like those who volunteer their time and labor at the Johnson City Crisis Center, we are laying the groundwork for a new American community.

CHAPTER
★ 15 ★

O ne of the most troubling results of the leadership of the current administration has been America's loss of standing in the world. Not only has President Bush isolated our country from many of our traditional allies, he has let America fall behind other countries in areas we should be leading—environmental practices, humanitarian aid, and public health, to name just a few. I believe that in order for America to remain strong in the future, we must once again become a nation that is not only feared but admired. We must restore our role as an idealistic moral force in the world.

When George W. Bush was running for president in 2000, he pledged a foreign policy based on humility. Instead, our foreign policy has ended up based on humiliation. After September 11, 2001, most of the world had such goodwill toward our country. One French newspaper carried a headline after the tragedy that read, "We Are All Americans Now." It is amazing to me how that goodwill has been completely squandered in just two years.

The outcome of elections in countries long allied to us, such as Germany and South Korea, have been affected by which candidate is more willing to stand up to oppose American policies. Increasing numbers of people in Europe, Asia, and in our own hemisphere cite America not as a pillar of freedom and democracy, but as a threat to peace. Our own soldiers are being targeted around the world, particularly those who were sent to Iraq.

I believe that the United States has a special role to play in world affairs. We have long been an inspiration to all those around the world seeking democracy, freedom, and opportunity. One of the reasons I decided to run for president is that we are squandering this legacy as the beacon of hope and justice for all humankind in favor of a new unilateralism even more dangerous than isolationism.

Americans are ready, I believe, to restore the best traditions of American leadership—leadership in which our power is multiplied by the appeal of democratic ideals and by the knowledge that our country is a force for law around the world, not a law unto itself.

I believe they are ready for leadership that would strive not to divide the world into "us versus them," but rather to rally the world around fundamental principles of decency, responsibility, freedom, and mutual respect. Our foreign and military policies must be about the notion of America leading the world, not America against the world.

From the time of its dedication in 1886, the Statue of Liberty remains the most potent symbol of freedom anywhere in the world. The statue is instantly recognizable and has, for more than a century, been synonymous with our country and our ideals. The statue's official name is "Liberty Enlightening the World," and that is precisely what we have been doing for most of our history. We remember the key part we played in helping to save democracy in both world wars when so many Americans sacrificed themselves so that we might live on in freedom. We recall the Marshall Plan which helped rebuild Europe after the war.

Presidents such as Truman, Eisenhower, and Kennedy built and strengthened international institutions, rather than dismissing and disparaging the concerns of allies. They inspired and mobilized other countries because they believed there was no more powerful force on earth than that of free people working together.

They helped build global platforms, such as the U.N., NATO, and the World Bank, on which free people everywhere could stand. Our greatest leaders built America's reputation as the world's leading democracy by never resting until they had given life to American ideals.

The Cold War was won in the 1980s because we in the United States not only proved our military strength but proved that we were a country to be admired. The Berlin Wall came down without a single shot being fired because people on the other side wanted to be like us, not because they were afraid of us. People in the Soviet Union and the Eastern bloc and beyond demanded a change within their own governments because we showed them, through the force of our moral example, what it meant to be a free people. Our moral example is part of our ability to lead and our ability to defend ourselves.

I opposed the war in Iraq because I believed then, as I believe now, that Iraq was not an imminent threat to the security of the United States. I believed that bullying other nations into joining us in a questionable war would divide much of the world against us. I disagree with the whole notion of preemptive war. I do not believe that it is a comprehensive strategy for addressing the threat that terrorists, tyrants, and technologies of mass destruction pose in the twenty-first century. If the doctrine is misused, it might well have the opposite effect from what is intended. I learned as a doctor that the first rule is: Do no harm. We certainly need to deal with the terrorist threat, but we have to lead by example and exercise power responsibly.

I also believed that devoting our resources to such a massive undertaking as an invasion and reconstruction of a country the size of California would harm our efforts in the war against terrorism—we simply cannot effectively do everything at once. I also believed that the United States might be seen not as liberators, but as conquerors, and that we might end up fueling the hatred of a whole new generation of terrorists.

In short, I opposed it because it was not in our best interests, nor was it based on our best ideals. I opposed the war and stood up against this administration, and even when 70 percent of the American people supported the war, I believed that the evidence was not there and refused to change my view.

In July 2003, there was a large furor over the president's now-famous State of the Union assertion, "The British government has learned that Saddam Hussein recently sought significant quantities of uranium from Africa"—the notorious "sixteen words." Of course it turned out that that statement was unsubstantiated—the evidence was discredited—and yet it was presented to the American people anyway. I was frankly stunned by these revelations. The American people were misled, and misled grievously.

At the time the sixteen words were being debated, I asked the administration sixteen questions that went to the heart of their justification of the war in Iraq. We wanted to know exactly how the sentence about Iraq going to the African nation of Niger to buy uranium had made it into the State of the Union address. We also heard in the address about "high-strength aluminum tubes suitable for nuclear weapons production" that could not really be used for that purpose. I also asked for concrete evidence that there were links between al-Qaeda and Iraq, which had been cited as a reason for attacking Iraq. Now the president has admitted that Saddam Hussein had nothing to do with the September 11 attacks. But it's far too late. The American people were led to that conclusion by the misleading statements of this administration, and after-the-fact admissions can't excuse that.

As commander-in-chief of the United States military, I will not hesitate to send our troops overseas to defend America. But as commander-in-chief of the military, I will never send our sons and daughters, brothers and sisters, in harm's way without telling the American people the truth about why they are going to war.

The search for weapons of mass destruction in Iraq continues as of this writing. Even if we find them, we deserve to know why we did not find them until many months after the Iraqi regime fell if they were supposedly an imminent threat and ready for imminent use. If these weapons are never found, then either the inspection regime was successful or they have been removed and may now be in the hands of terrorists. Each of these possibilities raises serious questions. In either case, we need to know the truth.

There was never any doubt that we would win the war once we engaged, and I fully supported our troops. While we won the war, we have not won the peace. We failed to plan for peace as we planned for war. The president rejected General Eric Shinseki's professional military advice that at least 200,000 troops would be needed. For many months there was no significant effort to bring in the international community—NATO or Arab and Islamic countries—to help stabilize Iraq.

In September, President Bush asked Congress for $87 billion for our military forces in Iraq and for reconstruction. Our unilateral occupation of Iraq has been costing $1 billion a week at a time of historic budget deficits. We must remember that the administration never wanted to tell the

American people what this war was going to cost and what we would be sacrificing.

In sum, this was the wrong war at the wrong time for our country. But, having been committed to it, we cannot afford to fail. Our first order of business must be to enlist the support and the assistance of our allies and the world community. And this is going to happen only if we agree to work with them as partners and to cede to them some of our control over the reconstruction. At this juncture, we do not have a choice. We cannot walk away and leave the situation worse than it was before. We cannot afford to continue to go it alone. We will always be stronger if we work in concert with the world and if our actions are always guided by the notion that we must lead by example and not simply by force.

Around the world, there exist a number of substantial threats to our national security. Those threats are not just military in nature. They are also in the form of environmental issues, disease, and poverty. Terrorism and rogue nations are grievous threats to our physical security, but our vision of security in the twenty-first century has to be much broader than before. If we do not view issues like AIDS and global warming as long-term threats, we are misunderstanding what it means to be secure in our interconnectedness. These global problems can only be addressed multilaterally and through alliances, and being the strongest military power in the world won't make us any more secure against the next SARS or other outbreak.

HOWARD DEAN

This consensus-building approach works for the more traditional security issues, as well. Take North Korea. The administration has failed to talk one-on-one with North Korea's leaders. This is a perfect example of a foreign policy characterized by petulance. I don't agree with the notion that just because you don't like someone, you shouldn't engage them in negotiation and dialogue. I think that giving them the stiff arm and pushing them away are only likely to isolate them further. Isolation can translate into dangerous belligerence.

In the Middle East, however, the administration's approach has failed in other ways. Because we've failed to reduce our dependence on oil from the Middle East, we have failed to confront countries such as Saudi Arabia about their ongoing financial support for terrorism. Because we've spurned our allies on other issues, we don't have the support we should from Europe or Russia in pressing the Iranians about their nuclear development program. I favor a tough stance toward all these countries—the Saudis, the Iranians, the Syrians, and others who send our oil money to Hamas and other terrorist organizations, which then finance a worldwide network of fundamentalist schools dedicated to teaching small children to hate Americans, Christians, Jews, and moderate Muslims.

Of course, the Israeli-Palestinian conflict remains at the center of much of the instability in the Middle East. A solution must be found, and the United States is really the only nation that can play the role of honest broker at the negotiating table in bringing that about. And the very reason this is true is the unique and special historic relationship we have with Israel and our guarantee of its defense and security. Because of that relationship, only we are well positioned to play the role of an honest broker to bring the sides together to find peace.

I deplore violence of any kind, especially violence perpetrated by terrorists against innocent civilians. And the Palestinians are going to have to take real action against the terrorist infrastructure that exists in their midst. But the truth is that real peace will require sacrifice and compromise on both sides, and a president of the United States ready to pick up where Bill Clinton left off and make this issue a top personal priority.

In the face of the ongoing spiral of violence, I have not lost hope. I know that the majorities of people on both sides of this conflict want peace and would agree to a reasonable two-state solution. I know how high their hearts were lifted over the past decade by the images of President Clinton hosting signing ceremonies for peace agreements at the White House. We must recapture that hope again, and only U.S. leadership can rekindle it.

We must reexamine, and renegotiate when necessary, the long list of multilaterally negotiated agreements rejected by the Bush administration: the Comprehensive Test Ban Treaty, the Kyoto Treaty, the Law of the Sea Treaty, the Biological Warfare Convention Protocol, the International Criminal Court, the Landmine Convention; the list goes on and on. These treaties are not without flaws, but the answer is to work to rewrite them, not to walk away from them.

We must also recognize the importance of spreading

the benefits of economic growth as widely as possible. The growth of multinational corporations and the globalization of the economy have helped create wealth and economic growth. But we must make certain that people in the developing world are full and equal beneficiaries in this growth.

As long as half the world's population subsists on less than $2 a day, the United States will not be secure. Poor states and failed states provide breeding grounds for disease as well as recruits and safe havens for terrorists. A world populated by "hostile have-nots" is not one in which U.S. leadership can be sustained without coercion.

In addition to supporting the growth of fair global trade, we must use our foreign assistance monies strategically to support the rule of law, combat corruption, help the most needy, and assist governments in creating democracies and developing infrastructure and human resources in their countries. We must bring still more energy to the cooperative battle against HIV/AIDS, which in too many countries is undermining security and tearing the heart out of economies, communities, and entire generations.

I have visited Africa and been extremely impressed by the public health education programs I saw there, both in cities and in the countryside. The educators are very skilled at talking with the people about public health.

We also learned recently that HIV-positive people in Africa might follow their drug regimens more closely than people in this country. In countries like Botswana, Uganda, Senegal, and South Africa, patients take about 90 percent of their pills compared with 70 percent in this country. It has been argued that there is no point in sending expensive antiretroviral drugs to Africa because people there don't abide by the regimen. This might be dangerous because it can promote drug-resistant strains of HIV. It turns out that patients in Africa might actually be more rather than less careful taking their drugs. While Africans have the will and the know-how, they do not have the resources. Clearly, the fight against HIV/AIDS is a global issue that must be tackled for everyone, by everyone.

We are part of the world community, and we must address the threat of global warming and do our part to control emissions that harm the global environment. We must step to the forefront and promote sustainable development. Instead of giving Americans incentives to conserve fuel, this administration says we should just drill for oil in the Arctic National Wildlife Refuge in Alaska. The Union of Concerned Scientists says that building more fuel-efficient cars could save more oil by 2012 than the Arctic National Wildlife Refuge could ever produce. We have lost the lead we once had in many areas of energy conservation. The administration weakened efficiency standards for air conditioners, for example. Fuel economy is lower than it has been in decades. In the early 1980s, California generated more than 80 percent of the world's wind power, but today that lead has been ceded to Europe, where three-quarters of this energy is generated.

I talked earlier about the hundred-year plans that we need to have when it comes to the environment. As I have gone around the country, there has been one Republican president I have been happy to give credit to. Theodore Roosevelt was president a hundred years ago, and he articulated a vision that has stood the test of time. The first time he saw the Grand Canyon, a place that is truly one of the natural wonders of the world, he asked that the people of Arizona work so that it remained unspoiled. "Leave it as it is," he said. "Keep it for your children and your children's children and for all who come after you, as one of the great sights which every American should see."

A hundred years later, the Bush administration wants to allow more logging in the Tongass National Forest in Alaska, the largest rain forest in the country. In a hundred years, will there be anything left for our children's children's children to see there?

We cannot ignore climate change, population growth, famine, or the many other global problems that we face. To address them, we must break free of the special interests that constrain our ability to tackle these serious problems.

Moral leadership begins at home. It is simply wrong for the United States to be the only developed country that does not guarantee health care to its citizens. We cannot credibly claim to be moral leaders when 41 million Americans still lack health insurance.

We must also deal honestly with the problem of poverty in America, the shrinking middle class, and the widening gap between the rich and poor. We cannot credibly denounce humanitarian shortcomings abroad without dealing with our own.

As John F. Kennedy said, we do these things not because

they are easy but because they are hard. The United States was once the beacon of hope in the world. We can be so again. The world has long looked to us as an example of how to behave. We must do our best to make sure the example we set inspires the world to race to the top, and not the bottom.

IN CLOSING

President Clinton, who was probably the greatest political mind in the White House since Franklin Roosevelt, once said that Americans would always vote for someone who is strong and wrong before they'd vote for someone who is weak and right. The problem for the Democratic Party in recent elections is how weak it has looked as it has strived to wrap its message in Republican-sounding packaging. Our problem isn't that the majority of the people in this country don't believe what we believe. To my mind, President Bush has been so popular because he sends such a clear and unambiguous message about where he wants to lead America. He connected with sections of the voting population because of the strength of his message—even though those same people didn't necessarily agree with him on the issues. He epitomizes "strong and wrong": strong because of the conviction with which he presents his case, and wrong because he is leading the country based on an ideological agenda that has little to do with what's best for the majority of Americans.

I know George W. Bush personally and the truth is, I don't think the president is particularly power-hungry. But I believe the people around him, people like Karl Rove, Dick Cheney, Donald Rumsfeld, Paul Wolfowitz, and Richard Perle, are. They have ridden to power behind a president who is focused and disciplined and said what he had to say to become president. I honestly believe he has little vision other than to keep himself and his party in power, and that desire has been exploited by a group of people with a dangerous ideological agenda.

On the other hand, the message of the Democratic Party in recent elections—largely constructed by pollsters and focus groups—may have been right on the merits, but has appeared weak and manufactured. When you are trying to satisfy political professionals rather than talking to the people, the people will see right through you. The people are smarter than that. Often, they're way out ahead of politicians in their thinking. I believe the Democratic Party must present a vision for America that represents a genuine alternative.

A lot of Democrats have given up on their party. Party leaders may regret the votes Ralph Nader attracted, but they haven't asked why we don't give the Nader voters a reason to turn out for us. In the same vein, we also haven't given young people much reason to vote. African-

Americans are the most loyal followers of the Democratic Party, and we haven't energized them or Latinos or labor unions for a long, long time. Some politicians in Washington apparently think we can take the Democratic base for granted and that somehow we'll be able to appeal to conservatives.

I disagree. With a strategy of always moving to the center, always sounding like Republicans, Democrats have made it possible for George W. Bush to move so far to the right, he's become the most radical president in our lifetime. By being afraid to stand up to the Republicans and their radical agenda, the Democrats have actually empowered the radical right. We've voted for the Republican agenda half the time in the belief that this somehow allows us to straddle the place where the votes are.

But I don't think the voters want George W. Bush's policies. I don't think they want me-tooism, either. More than anything else, they want someone to stand up to George W. Bush, explain to the American people why he is wrong, and treat them like adults.

In my June 23 announcement speech, I quoted Martin Luther King, Jr., who said, "Our lives begin to end the day we become silent about things that matter." We have to be positive and lay out an agenda that challenges the mean-spiritedness and cruelty of the Republican right, which commands the three branches of government in America today. We've got to stand up for our human values, for our dignity, for our community, and for our respect for one another once again. Our vision of America is one based on hope and based on the responsibility we have for one another.

President Bush can command a lot of wealthy corporate contributors. But there are millions and millions of Americans who are left out of the political process and can be brought back in. These are people who have been disillusioned with Washington, people who believed their vote didn't make a difference. These are people like those at the rally in Seattle who raised their hand and indicated they hadn't been involved in politics for ten or fifteen years.

I want to finish where I began, with my announcement speech in Burlington. The themes I talked about that day run through this book. I am not going to tell any American that I can solve all their problems. The power is in your hands.

The truth is the future of our nation rests in your hands, and not in mine. Abraham Lincoln said that government of the people, by the people, and for the people shall not perish from this earth.

But this president has forgotten ordinary people.

You have the power to reclaim our nation's destiny.

You have the power to rid Washington of the politics of money.

You have the power to make right as important as might.

You have the power to restore our nation to fiscal sanity and bring jobs back to our people.

You have the power to fulfill Harry Truman's dream and
   bring health insurance to every American.
You have the power to give us a foreign policy consistent
   with American values again.
You have the power to take back the Democratic Party.
And you have the power to take our country back.